P9-DGM-715

A MAN'S GARDEN

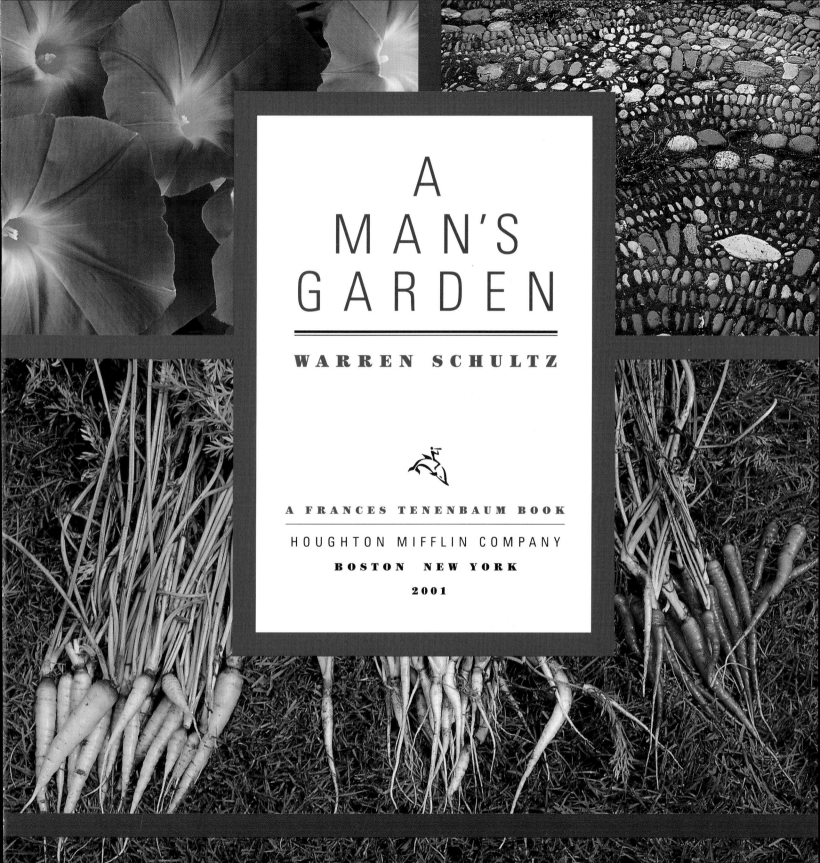

A
MAN'S
GARDEN

WARREN SCHULTZ

A FRANCES TENENBAUM BOOK

HOUGHTON MIFFLIN COMPANY

BOSTON NEW YORK

2001

Copyright © 2000 by Warren Schultz

All rights reserved

For information about permission to reproduce selections from
this book, write to Permissions, Houghton Mifflin Company,
215 Park Avenue South, New York, New York 10003.

Visit our Web site: www.houghtonmifflinbooks.com

Library of Congress Cataloging-in-Publication Data

Schultz, Warren.
    A man's garden / Warren Schultz.
        p. cm.
    "A Frances Tenenbaum book."
    ISBN 0-618-00392-4
    1. Gardening — United States.   2. Gardeners —
United States.   I. Title.

SB455 .S35 2001
635'.0973—dc21   00-061330

Book design by Anne Chalmers
Typefaces: ITC Century, Universe Condensed

Printed in Italy
SFE 10 9 8 7 6 5 4 3 2 1

TO MY MOM, ROSEMARY,

who has lived her life in the company of gardening men

AND TO MY DAD, WARREN SR.,

who planted the love of gardening in me

ACKNOWLEDGMENTS

I'd like to offer thanks to everyone who took an interest in my quest and helped me track down these gardens, including Tovah Martin, Erica Glasener, Virginia Weiler, Dency Kane, Charles Mann, Susan Seubert, and Cathy Vail. A special thanks to Allison Mia Starcher for her support and encouragement. Thanks to my daughters, Emme and Zea, for bearing with me during the book-writing process, and to their mother for carrying more than her share of the load. I'd like to offer a heartfelt thanks to my editor, Frances Tenenbaum, for her patience and good humor.

CONTENTS

ix

A MAN'S GARDEN

Guys dig color, and lots of it. Many a man's garden features great masses of bright, primary-colored flowers.

INTRODUCTION

Some men garden to build monuments to themselves and their masculine industriousness.

I'M TIRED OF BEING TOLD that gardening is woman's work. I don't like the way my buddies roll their eyes when I tell them I'd rather weed a border than watch a hockey game between Saskatoon and Moose Jaw, but there's no shame in being a gardening man. Farmers? Men. Landscape architects? Men. Golf-course greenskeepers? Men. Plant breeders? Men. How did the garden come to be seen as a woman's domain? It's not, you know. There are 36 million male gardeners in America, a strong cadre of real men with manly gardens. Granted, for many of them the landscape begins at the sidewalk and ends at the front steps, and in between there's nothing but green, green grass. Hauling out the mower every Saturday is the extent of their "gardening."

But plenty of men are real gardeners, who subscribe to a masculine style of planting. Is there such a thing as a man's garden? You can bet your last six-pack there is. In fact, there are several archetypal styles of men's gardens, whose plants or design or furnishings satisfy certain basic needs of a man's psyche. Some men's gardens are playful, others are competitive. Some are places to fool with tools.

1

The big, square, straight-row back-yard vegetable garden is classically a man's territory, where he can fulfill the need to provide for his family.

Many have decks and hammocks and built-in barbecue pits. There might be a bocce court, a putting green, or even a quiet corner where a man can sit and enjoy a cigar. A man's garden may have vegetables, and if it does, it certainly has tomatoes—monster tomatoes, the biggest on the block. It may have a tall and unruly flower border in a riot of colors. It probably has some old-fashioned, unfashionable flowers. It may have cactuses or hedges or a collection of roses or dahlias.

To me, the idea of testosterone in the garden seems natural. I grew up surrounded by gardening men. Well, they weren't exactly gardening. This was not a leisure-time activity or a hobby; it was serious business. These guys were farmers—shirt-sleeves-rolled-up, cigarette-smoking, work-boot-wearing, wisecracking guys: my dad, my uncle, my cousins. The men worked the fields, the women kept house and planted little flower gardens beside the back door.

My father was the greatest influence on me. You had to take only one look at him to be assured that gardening was a manly activity. Six feet tall, 250 pounds, he was an all-city high school football player who attended Notre Dame on an athletic scholarship. In time, though, he gave up his scholarship to return home and help his mother run the family farm.

A man does his duty. He takes care of his family, he

works the soil. Those were the unspoken rules I learned as a child. And from the time I was twelve I worked beside my father, growing vegetables. The business changed with the times, and eventually he expanded the farm to include a greenhouse and a nursery. To some, growing pansies might seem less manly than growing corn, but he took to it easily. You could count on my dad being up at dawn every day and at work not long afterward. You would find him in the greenhouse, walking the aisles with a hose in his hand, whistling some dumb show tune.

Every spring Dad would set aside an evening to plant a flower garden beside the road. I'm sure he told himself that this was a marketing ploy. That ornamental garden of annuals would catch the eyes of passersby and show off our flowering goods to their best advantage.

It was always the same garden. He would plow a long, straight, narrow strip, rake it smooth, and mark it out with strings. He'd start by planting a long straight row of red cannas right down the center of the bed. On either side he put a row of 'Apollo' marigolds, then a row of red salvia, a row of shorter marigolds, and finally, a row of red geraniums. It was bright. It was straight. It was symmetrical and simple. It was red and orange and yellow. People would drive by and, sure enough, some would stop to ask about those tall red flowers. Most of those people were men.

That roadside garden attracted attention just as it was supposed to and completely satisfied my dad. It didn't matter that there wasn't an unusual plant in it, not a single

A man likes to make a splash with his garden. If he's going to have a perennial border, then, by God, it will be the longest in the neighborhood.

curve or surprise to be found. And, after spending all day hoeing long straight rows of peppers or tomatoes, Dad would be in that garden at dusk on his knees, pulling weeds from between the rows of flowers.

Over the years, my own gardens have had some of my father in them. Oh, sure, they've had raised beds and mulch and perennials as well, but they're usually built around vegetables, and there's always a bright red canna or two in there somewhere.

Men love annuals, from bright red geraniums to garish marigolds to multicolored snapdragons. Annuals are simple. We don't need to fuss over them or divide them. We plant them on Memorial Day every year, fertilize, water, and weed when necessary, and we have blooms all summer. Those are the kinds of results that men love. Maybe we identify just a bit with those bright annual flowers. We're loud. We're a little awkward. We like to call atten-

Railroad gardening has caught on in a big way with men. It satisfies the urge to create a world of their own while allowing them to play with toys.

tion to ourselves. We may lack subtlety, but we like to think we're constant and low-maintenance.

Men also love exotics—cactus, palms, and orchids. We love the hunt involved in tracking down rare species. We love the challenge of growing plants out of their natural element. Most of all, we love the joy of showing them off.

Men love lawns and hedges—any plant that needs to be chopped, pruned, and trimmed. We like the feeling of power that comes from hacking away at a plant to keep it under control.

Men love vegetables. We love the idea of growing our own food, even if that food is four hundred pounds of zucchini and a couple of ears of corn. We love the idea that we are providers. Growing vegetables is worthwhile and manly because we are putting food on the table for our family, hearkening back to an earlier time in our country.

The United States began as an agrarian nation, which may explain why the tradition of hobby gardening for men is not as strong here as it is in Europe. In our not too distant past, gardening meant farming, and farming was hard work, a hardscrabble existence. You didn't grow plants for relaxation unless you belonged to the privileged class. Farming has been seen as a form of labor to rise above, the agrarian life something to escape from. For hundreds of years American farmers have struggled so that their sons could have a better life. But today, millions of American men garden. And they do so for many reasons.

TO RECAPTURE THE PAST. Many men garden to satisfy an urge to return to the solid ground of childhood, when life was simple and Dad had all the answers. In the garden it's easy to let go of current problems and fall into the comfort of the past. The warm, wet soil smells the same as it did thirty years ago. The freshly picked green beans still taste like the ones picked from Dad's garden. These guys' gardens tend to be filled with old-fashioned plants in long straight rows.

TO SATISFY THE NEED FOR ORDER. Gardens are predictable. We know the grass needs mowing every week. We know the hedge needs trimming monthly. We know the tomatoes will ripen in ninety days. We can be certain the Japanese beetles will find the roses. Some men take comfort in that predictability. Their landscapes are often marked by neatly trimmed lawns and weed-free flower beds.

TO CONTROL. Sometimes we feel as if our lives are spinning out of control. But in the garden we can take control. We can cut the trees into weird shapes. We can blast the bugs when they dare to attack our prized plants. We can water and feed to make them grow. And we can yank out every single weed that dares to invade our plot. In short, we can become the masters of our back-yard universe.

TO PROVIDE A PLACE TO PLAY. As we grow older, our playgrounds disappear. Our lives fill up with work and duty, and time for relaxation diminishes. For many men, the garden is the only place to putter, play with tools, put together projects. These guys often fill their gardens with toys, sports courts, or whimsical yard art.

TO ESCAPE. These days most of us spend our lives surrounded by steel and asphalt, cut off from nature by sealed windows. The garden is one of the few places that allows us an escape, where we can come face to face with nature, even if it's in the form of hybridized, domesticated plants. Guys who garden to get back in touch with nature often choose native plants for their gardens.

TO MAKE A MARK. Even to this day, the interior of the house is likely to be a woman's domain. A man may not have much to say about the style of the curtains or bedding. But outdoors a guy can decide what to plant around the deck or how short to trim the flowering shrubs. He can plant trees, carve beds out of the lawn, or grow giant pumpkins. In short, he can make the garden his own outdoor room.

TO SATISFY A COMPULSION. In some cases, a man just gets carried away. He spots a certain plant and it speaks to him. He discovers a particular gardening style that resonates deep within him. Before he knows it, his yard is overrun with cactuses or palms or some other plant that inspires his passion. Often he can't even explain why he collects the plant. He only knows he has to.

TO CREATE. Some men need to shape the world around them, even if it's only a small part of the world. They seize the opportunity to move dirt, dig holes, change views, and create their own sanctuary.

In the end, there may be as many reasons to garden and as many gardening styles as there are gardeners. On the pages that follow, you'll visit a few outstanding and diverse gardens created and maintained by men. There are vegetable gardens, flower gardens, small gardens, grand gardens. They have little in common, except that each one satisfies a particular man's passion. Each is a perfectly realized example of what that man thinks a garden should be.

RALPH VELEZ

WESTMINSTER, CALIFORNIA

**The slow-growing triangle palm,
Dypsis decaryi, a native of
Madagascar, has a place of honor
in front of the Velez house.**

FOR MANY MEN, the garden is a place to hide. That seems to be true for Ralph Velez of Westminster, California. It's easy to get literally lost in his yard, because this suburban lot is a jungle crammed with towering palm trees and an understory of other tropical plants.

Ralph Velez, a New York City transplant blooming in southern California, has created an awe-inspiring collection of palms. He has 483 of them growing—no, not just growing, thriving—on a 60-by-150-foot corner lot. He hasn't done it the easy way, planting hundreds of specimens of a common species such as the royal palm. No, his collection comprises 370 different species: royal palm, queen palm, fishtail palm, coconut palm, potato-chip palm. It is one of the three largest private palm collections in the United States. And it looks great! No ragtag bunch of plants, it is a subtropical landscape surrounding, and sometimes overrunning, the home where he and his wife, Nilda, live.

Why has this high school art teacher devoted the past twenty years of his life to these plants? Perhaps because he knows how: his landscape represents his accomplishments grown huge. Palms germinated from tiny seeds or purchased as 99-cent plants now tower over the neighborhood. He sees them every day, as do his neighbors and his wife. Even though she doesn't share his passion, she can't deny that he has succeeded.

Sometimes a man's gotta do what a man's gotta do, even if his helpmate does not share his passion. Perhaps that's part of the attraction. Maybe a man wouldn't be so feverish about his garden if he had to share it with his partner, maybe he embraces this obsession because it is his alone.

It separates him from her, allows him his own world, and ultimately permits him to defy her in a harmless little way. Because she makes it clear, in no uncertain terms, that she thinks his passion is ridiculous.

No suburban landscape could make more of a personal statement than Ralph Velez's. You can spot his "garden" from blocks away. A dozen royal palm trees tower over everything in the neighborhood. Just point your car in that direction, and you'll find the Velez house. Well, you won't find the house right away because it's completely hidden by the plants.

Nilda thinks the house may be a little *too* easy to find. Ever since they were featured in a newspaper article and on a TV program, curious gardeners have made their way to the house in a steady stream. That's why you'll see "Keep Out" signs on the garage. It's not that the Velezes aren't friendly. It's not that they don't appreciate the atten-

(Left) Ralph's collection of hundreds of palms has outgrown his own yard, so he plants some, like this *Roystonea oleracea*, a royal palm from Jamaica, in his neighbors' yards.

(Above) You can spot Ralph's place from miles away. Just look for the 70-foot-tall Mexican fan palms. Ralph bought six of them in one-gallon containers and planted them in 1983.

tion of plant lovers. It's just that visitors arrive day and night, expecting a personal tour of the grounds. "Enough is enough," says Nilda.

Those who are invited in have a treat in store. Ralph is eager and excited to show off his love, and Nilda, despite her lack of enthusiasm for the plants, is a gracious hostess. They gladly take the time to chat over tea and cookies before leading the nickel tour of the grounds.

On the back patio, sitting deep in the shade of the palm jungle, you can easily forget that you are surrounded by houses. The yard wasn't always like this. Once there were other plants here, and a lawn that flowed into the neighbor's lawn. There were even some fruit trees once upon a time.

Velez, a slight, wiry man with thinning white hair and an ever-present smile, came to gardening late. He grew up in an apartment in Queens, the son of an immigrant from Puerto Rico. (If you listen carefully you can still hear a New York accent when he gets excited.) There really was zero gardening in that household. But Ralph was fascinated by the tropics, by "jungle plants," by stories his father told him about Puerto Rico.

"Growing up I never did any gardening," Velez says. But he remembers his first plant, which he and Nilda brought back from their honeymoon in Puerto Rico. "It was an *Areca* palm," he explains, "very common in the tropics. I wanted to bring it home, but I was told you can't take soil. So I washed all the soil off and brought it back in a plastic bag with water. At home I potted it up and we had it in our house on Long Island." That was about the extent of Ralph's gardening in New York. "Even though we had a house with a yard, I still didn't do much planting. Eventually the neighbors complained because I never planted the back yard. I was really busy. I planted the front and that was it."

One problem was the New York climate. After Velez visited Puerto Rico, he realized that he wanted to live in a climate that was at least semitropical. He and Nilda thought about Miami, Puerto Rico, and Arizona before settling on southern California.

They bought a house on a corner lot in Westminster, and Ralph started landscaping. "When we found this lot, the house was just being built," he explains. "We moved in in February or March, and once it stopped raining there was mud everywhere. But I started planting. I put in a lawn in the front [now gone]. I put a lawn in the back [gone]. We put in apricots, oranges, avocadoes [all gone, replaced by palms]. I purchased some ferns and philodendrons [a few still remain in the shadow of palms]. But it wasn't long before I started going directly toward palms."

He soon realized that the other plants were taking up space that could be devoted to palms. He wanted enough palms to cover the ground, hide the house, and create a tropical feel.

He remembers the moment when he (and his wife) real-

There's barely enough room to squeeze a car into the driveway between palms, including the Mexican Bahia palm, right.

A MAN'S GARDEN

ized that his love for palms had become a passion. "Stop calling it an obsession," he says to Nilda. "It's a passion."

As in most cities, the grassy strips between the sidewalk and the street in Westminster are usually "landscaped" with turf and a few scattered (and invariably struggling) trees. Ralph didn't like the single messy pepper tree that had been planted by the parks department right in front of his house. After all, it clashed with his young tropical landscape. So early one morning he cut it down and replaced it with a palm.

Nilda had a fit. She thought the tree police would come and arrest them, but they didn't. And when they didn't, Ralph grew bold and planted another palm, and then another. Eventually someone from the city did come by. He and Ralph had a nice talk about palms. The parks man said he liked they way they looked, and that was all Ralph needed to hear. "I said, 'Can I continue planting palms in

Ralph's son, Steve, has caught the bug from his dad and is also an avid palm collector.

the circle?' He said, 'Yeah, sure.' So I planted a few more and a few more. Now there are palms planted along the entire circle. I just knock on everybody's door and ask if I can plant in front of their house."

Eventually he moved beyond the sidewalk strip. Now he plants his palms smack in the middle of neighbors' yards (with their permission, of course). His lot is so full and so shady that he has to find other garden space for the sun-loving palms. He gazes longingly at a neighbor's sunny lawn, envisioning how a palm would look there, how fast it would grow. He finally gets up the nerve and asks if he can plant. Usually the neighbor says sure, fine. So he does.

9

Ralph's yard, home to hundreds of palms, including the Dr. Seuss–like *Nannorrhops ritchiana,* at left, also contains many other tropical plants, including tree ferns, right, and ligularia, center.

A MAN'S GARDEN

Then he wrings his hands as he sees the owner neglect it or nick it with the lawn mower.

His own yard has no room for anything else, but he keeps planting seeds in his greenhouse. "I just got a package in from Hawaii. My wife says, 'Where are you gonna put 'em?' and I say, 'I always find room.' I make room. I'll never stop collecting and germinating seed."

Nilda, in the meantime, tends a single spindly little tomato plant, exiled to the edge of the lot, near the driveway. In this place, Ralph is the boss, the king of the castle grounds. "My wife wanted roses," he explains. "I said 'You don't put roses in a tropical garden!'" You can still hear the outrage in his voice. "But I relented. I grew a few roses along the driveway for her for a few years, and then they just died."

Nilda is not much into gardening herself. "It was not part of the culture," she says. "Growing up in Puerto Rico I was never allowed to play in the mud. I was never allowed to get my hands dirty. I still don't feel right about it."

But she allows Ralph his palms and the time they require. He fusses over them, coaxing seedlings from tiny seeds in his greenhouse, labeling every plant with date and size and origin. He hires someone with a cherry picker to remove seeds from the Mexican fan palms and hangs nets high in the trees to catch the fronds from the king palm as they fall, lest they damage the smaller palms. A single coconut palm gets the most attention—"because growing a coconut palm in California is next to impossible to do," as Ralph says. He is growing it in a makeshift hothouse—a plastic-covered planter with a heating element to keep the soil temperature about eighty degrees. He is bursting with pride as he shows it off.

Ralph is obviously proud of his collection and his skill in maintaining it. He's also gratified by his role as mentor to many neophyte palm growers. "A friend just got into palms about a year ago. And now he's going out of his mind growing thousands of them," he says. "He called the other day to tell me he just germinated some very rare palms and that's he's so indebted to me."

Ralph often hosts meetings of the local chapter of the Palm Society, and he gives tours to local groups. Nilda thinks it's all a bit much. "She's not much on having people over anymore. She used to go to meetings with me, used to go to the banquet with me, but I can't get her to do that now."

He doesn't seem too bothered by her lack of interest in palms. It is, after all, *his* passion.

THE OBSESSED

PEARL FRYAR

BISHOPVILLE, SOUTH CAROLINA

YOU **THINK YOU KNOW TOPIARY?** Even if you've seen the boxwood fox hunt at Ladew Topiary Gardens, marveled at the creatures at Green Animals in Rhode Island or the topiary cartoon characters at Disney World, you've never seen anything like Pearl Fryar's yard in Bishopville, South Carolina. As marvelous as those other plant sculptures are, they seem rather stiff and uninspired once you've seen Pearl's.

(Above) Pearl's trademark, a 20-foot-tall Leyland cypress fishbone, towers over his yard and stops traffic in the neighborhood.

(Left) It takes a tall ladder and a lot of time for Pearl Fryar to maintain the collection of nearly five hundred topiary plants on his South Carolina property.

12

A MAN'S GARDEN

No telling what you might find in Pearl Fryar's back yard. Here a tribute to a diet cola has been fashioned of plants and stone. Why? Because the jingle stuck in his head

Pearl's yard contains nearly five hundred trees and shrubs pruned to marvelous, often indescribable shapes. There are curves and spires and spikes, and even letters and words, carved out of all manner of trees and shrubs. If it's a plant, Pearl will prune it.

It's hard to believe that when Pearl started carving up greenery, he had never even heard the word "topiary." In a very real sense, he didn't know what he was doing. Pearl just "got a hankering" to take the shears to a shrub. And once he started, he couldn't stop. He had a vision, and that vision became an obsession.

Picture Richard Dreyfuss sculpting a mesa out of mashed potatoes in the movie *Close Encounters of the Third Kind*. Remember the palpable sense of obsession? Remember how it was just a little bit scary to think that someone was obeying an inner voice? Observe Pearl Fryar in the garden, and you get that same feeling. Pearl is obsessed, not with gardening in general, but with one very specific and quirky form of gardening.

"Obsessed" is a word we toss around pretty freely: he is obsessed with his tomato plants; she is obsessed with her roses. But most of the time we just mean that the person enjoys the activity. A real obsession is when you feel compelled to dedicate your life to a discipline, even if you don't know its name. Such was the case for Pearl Fryar.

Pearl is a tall black man with bulging forearms, warm brown eyes, and a wide grin. He does not fit the profile of the typical topiary aficionado. Raised in the South, he moved to New York City and got a job on the production line for the American Can Company. It wasn't until he moved back to South Carolina in the early 1980s that he even thought about gardening. "Until I started this garden, I never even lived on the ground floor," he says. "I lived in an apartment in Queens, New York, for twelve years. Then I moved to an apartment in Atlanta. When we came back to Bishopville, we lived on the second floor for the first four years."

Pearl says he's always been looking for something to fulfill him. "I was a coin collector. I restored cars. I was constantly looking for the thing that would allow me to express myself. But I never found anything that gave me the personal satisfaction that gardening does.

"When I finally built my house here, I said, 'I think I'm gonna make me a nice garden. I'm not going anywhere for

a while.'" So he started looking around for ideas. While shopping for plants at a local nursery, he spotted a small holly topiary. Curious, he asked the nurseryman how it was done and received a crash course in basic pruning.

So Pearl bought a small plant and a pair of hand pruners and went to work. He clipped a leaf or two here, a branch or two there, and he was pretty satisfied with how it turned out. He kept clipping, observing how the plant reacted to each cut, and once he thought he had it figured out, he bought a second plant to work on.

Of course, his knowledge of pruning and plant growth was rudimentary after that short introduction at the nursery. But he says that ignorance worked to his advantage. "Since I had no horticultural background, I didn't set any

For the most part, Pearl shuns topiary animals as too ordinary, but you'll find a few roaming through the abstract shapes in his land-scape.

14

limits on what I could or couldn't do. People who know horticulture say you can't do the kind of pruning that I do, but I didn't know any better."

Somehow Pearl knew what to do once he had a a pair of clippers in his hand. Or at least he knew what he *wanted* to do. So he continued working with bigger and more diverse plants, planting them all over the yard. The creative act and the green result spoke to him at some deep level. There was nothing to do but go back and buy another plant and another, and keep pruning in his own inimitable style.

"My topiary is totally different from what you see anywhere else," Pearl says. "And it's not the kind of thing that can be copied. I like to expose the trunk and branches in relation to foliage. When you look at the plant the first thing you see is what I've done to the trunk."

After a few years of cutting and carving and planting, word spread about the guy with the strange plants in his yard. When a local horticulturist stopped by to talk about topiary, Pearl asked, "What's topiary?"

Once he learned that what he was doing had a name and a history, Pearl found a book on the subject and brought it out to the back yard. With the book in one hand and a pair of pruners in the other, he started to follow the instructions. It just didn't feel right, though. Pruning by the book, according to someone else's aesthetics, seemed too rigid. It was not personal enough. So he put the book on a shelf and went back to his own self-taught technique.

Pearl's method involves incorporating lines and curves into a rhythmic pattern that only he seems to understand.

He struggles to explain the personal creative rules he follows. "I always try to work a curve against a straight line to give me contrast," he says. "I cut flowing shapes instead of cutting round and square like most people do. Once I cut the first line in that plant, it's a matter of connecting lines and shoots. Eventually I'll come up with a shape."

Technically, his pruning method is very different from traditional topiary, which relies on the greenery of evergreen plants to create shapes. Pearl is not afraid to bare the trunk and let the wood become an element in the design. He does other things that traditional topiarists never would, such as using coat hangers to space the limbs and tying branches to hold them in position.

Pearl works with almost all kinds of plants, including hollies, junipers, Leyland cypress, blue spruce, Alberta spruce, even oaks and pyracantha. His equipment includes ladders, floodlights for working at night, and gas-

Pearl will shape just about any plant, including pyracantha, into his own personal vision.

15

Pearl has carved a 250-foot-long border out of Leyland cypress and upright junipers, and every plant takes a different shape, he points out proudly.

powered hedge shears. With so much work to do and so many shrubs to keep in line, he had to switch from hand tools to power tools.

Pearl cuts often. "I prune every three to four weeks," he says. "If you want to try pruning once or twice a year, that's fine. But you won't have topiary. You must cut before the plants become woody, or you won't control the size." Ask him why he spends so much time working with his plants, and his answer is simple. "I get visitors all the time. I've got to keep it presentable."

And what about those shapes? You might think that Pearl must spend a lot of time planning and sketching them out. Wrong—none of his designs spend any time on paper. They all go directly from his head (or his heart) to the garden. "They just come to me," he says, sounding a bit mystified by the process. I have a thousand shapes in my head."

A lot of those shapes make it into the garden. A long topiary border surrounds a heart-shaped annual bed. "And each plant is cut into a different shape," he points out. "You stand there and look, and you see all these abstract shapes in hollies and cypress and evergreens, and they all seem connected somehow."

All day long, while he's at work, fantastic shapes dance through his head. In the evening he makes them real. It is as though he is receiving a message from some other-worldly source and conveying that message in a strange green language.

"Everything around my house is totally different," Pearl says proudly. "I didn't copy a thing out of magazines or books. I don't care what other gardeners say. I don't care what the books say. I use the same plants that everyone else uses. But my garden does not look the same as everyone else's."

As you walk around, you can't help but notice a message; many of the trees are trimmed into hearts, and some are sculpted to form the word "Love." "I came out of the sixties," Pearl says. "I was part of that Woodstock generation. I've got that caring feeling deep down inside me. And I get along quite well with people who were considered hippies."

Pearl creates a lot of scenes that no one else would, and some might seem a bit, well, tacky, to others. But he doesn't care. "I garden for myself. One of my most favorite scenes in my garden is the Diet Pepsi 'uh huh' jingle made out of border grass and marble and pebbles with a fountain in the center."

Yes, it sounds strange. But you have to see it. You have to feel the garden around you and, preferably, see it with Pearl beside you, beaming about his creations.

"It's pop art," Pearl insists. "It's like Andy Warhol with the soup can. It gives you a sense of time in my garden, because if you remember that Pepsi commercial, then you'll know when my garden was created." The message doesn't have to be as obvious as that to move people, Pearl says. It just has to be plants cut into funny or harmonious shapes. "It amazes me what a shaped plant will do to people, even adults," he says.

He is still dumbfounded by the attention his garden garners. "I've been called a self-taught artist," he says. "Someone filmed a documentary about me." And he's often called on to give demonstrations. He has a thirty-minute slide show showing the trees in his landscape. "And it blows my mind," he says. "I get ovations for shapes of plants."

Now his yard is a regular stop on the obsessive-compulsive gardeners' circuit. The curious come from as far as Sweden to see Pearl's unique take on topiary. Pearl finds it incredibly rewarding to see people responding enthusiastically to his vision. People understand that those shapes created out of yew and cypress and holly are products of fervor and love.

Pearl doesn't think the appeal of his work is so mysterious. "Folks just want something different," he says. "They're tired of the same things over and over again."

Pearl's creations, resembling surreal sculptures, don't start with a particular kind of plant, he says. They just appear in his head as he works.

Doug Mayhew calls this his American temple. Cast-iron Federal-period columns, strung with morning glories and gourds, are surrounded by Turkish jars, French columns, and all manner of plants, including castor bean and acanthus.

DOUG MAYHEW

A clearing beside the river features nineteenth-century glazed stoneware. The small water garden, with cattails, iris, and *Pontederia cordata*, is surrounded by shrubs, including Carolina allspice, star magnolia, and oakleaf hydrangea.

WHEN YOU COME UPON the four massive Corinthian columns in a clearing in the brush, you know this is a man's garden. If you have any doubts after that, they will certainly be erased when you see the huge, rusted, banged-up iron gates that spring up in the middle of nowhere.

The undeniably, unapologetically phallic nature of those Greek columns and the massive scale and grand ambition stamp Doug Mayhew's creation as a man's garden. Trained in art, not horticulture, Mayhew is something of an outsider, who has crept into garden design and made the field his own. His firm, Mayhew/Orion, is one of the hot new East Coast, design-and-build shops, and his designs are as much art as they are horticulture. You might even call them installations. Here at his own home, as well as for his clients, he integrates his two loves, art and nature, into fully formed, attention-getting creations.

These are no sissified, "conceptual" installations. A lot of bulldozing, earthmoving, digging, and hauling go into creating them. And Mayhew, a wiry and muscular forty-something guy with sharp features and hair curling over his collar, is always right there at the bulldozer controls or with his hands wrapped around the handle of a spade. He's a hands-on guy. Besides the obvious muscle involved, there's usually some sort of mystery or even a horticultural prank evident in his work. That male humor may come from odd combinations of materials or tensions between plants.

19

Mayhew has given plenty of thought to men in the garden. "I think, because men tend to approach things on a scale that's always a little ahead of their capabilities, men's gardens tend to balance precariously between intimately personal and grandiose." He smiles when he says this, aware that his own garden is pushing the bounds of grandiose. "Changing the landscape is, of course, the dream of every kid who ever threw buckets of sand out of a sandbox or surveyed the world from a limb high in a tree."

He likes moving dirt. His four-acre riverside property in northwestern Connecticut was as flat as a Manhattan sidewalk when he bought it. Not satisfied with that situation, he brought in truckload after truckload of fill and topsoil to sculpt the land, to make hillocks and terraces. "It's not unusual for us to move sixty tons of dirt in a day," he says. And he's not the type to just stand and point. "When we're

Mayhew's garden is a jumble of stoneware, ironwork, garden antiques, and plants both native and exotic. This spot contains sedum 'Autumn Joy', *Rosa rugosa* 'Rubra', sempervirens, *Hydrangea macrophylla* 'Summer Beauty', *Hydrangea paniculata* 'Tardia', and three lilacs: 'Firmament', 'Katherine Havemeyer', and 'Madame Lemoine'.

Some of the most intriguing spots on Mayhew's property are the simplest. Here a nineteenth-century Portuguese jar sits on a concrete chimney block, framed by eastern hemlock and eastern white pine.

At the end of the day Doug likes to sit on his old metal glider and watch the Housatonic River flow by. The container garden features *Helichrysum variegatum* in the center, *Passiflora* 'Saint Rule', various moonflowers growing up supports, and agave, aloe vera, and euphorbia.

digging holes, I'm the one who's down in the hole."

Mayhew brings a sculptor's attitude to the garden. If you can imagine it, you can do it. Along the way he may break a lot of rules, but he's always been a plantsman at heart.

"I grew up in a family of tree planters and tree huggers," Doug says. "We had the good fortune to live in a forest in Michigan. It had natural features like swamps and bogs. And I was always a *National Geographic* kind of kid. I had a real natural-science bent toward geology, water, environment. I thought everyone grew up that way. My family had a reverence for the environment," he adds. "We spent a lot of hours in the car going on family trips, and they were always to points of natural beauty, like to see the big redwoods in California."

He comes from a long line of plant people. "My grandparents were into botany, too. My grandmother was one of the first female masters in science at the University of Michigan. She passed that interest on to us, and I guess some of it stuck."

Stuck like a thick glob of oil paint on a canvas. For nearly twenty years, though, as an artist and gallery manager in Manhattan, Mayhew had no garden. He got his dose of nature in Central Park. During that time he began noticing and appreciating the urban metaphors for nature and the natural metaphors for city life. "A lot of the garden design work I do now relates to my urban existence," he says. "I saw the skyscrapers of New York as the great redwoods of California. The rushing traffic of the city was a metaphor for the rushing rivers of Michigan."

Finally he decided to leave his gallery job and start a landscape design firm. Just like that—sort of like leaping into a midlife crisis. Now, just a few years after leaving the art world for the landscape world, he has put his name, and his very personal stamp, on estate gardens across the United States and even South America.

That should come as no surprise, really. He's a natural. This is the career he's been working toward all his life. He feels that he did not find his true calling until he melded sculpture with plants.

"I found that the connection between sculpture and gardening was the most natural I've ever made," he says. "I grew up in an age of conceptual art. I grew up admiring

A MAN'S GARDEN

artists like Robert Smithson. Sculptors who manipulated the land rang true to me. So a lot of my works were land based."

It was only a matter of time until he started moving plant material along with the earth. "So the tree-garden-plant thing is such a natural step. I started by manipulating the land, and then what occurred to me was to incorporate living things, material that grew and changed. There's such a phenomenal variety open to us. Those plants became colors in the palette."

There is one more factor in the equation, along with earth and plants, and that is steel. "When I finally really focused and saw the kind of landscape I wanted to create, I realized I would have to fabricate my own steelwork in order to create these vistas. So I built a studio and started welding." Since then his gardens have featured hard, bright, tall steel elements that definitely lend a masculine air. "In the end, what a lot of people put underground, I put aboveground. I show the bones, the metal, the stone. Garden armatures that others might generate from wood, I generate out of steel. I work with I-beams, angle irons, industrial materials. They were created for one purpose, but in my vocabulary they come out differently."

Part of the appeal of the material is its structure and strength. And part is simply that the color and texture of steel are rarely found in a garden.

"The steel starts out as an incredible gray, but as time passes it rusts and changes," Doug says. "Maybe after one

hundred years it will have rusted away entirely. In the meantime, though, the steel integrates itself into the garden in a great way." The same way an old plow or disk harrow becomes part of the environment of an abandoned New England farm.

Mayhew has given plenty of thought to the source of fascination with steel and structure. "I believe that my need to make huge structures goes back to a childhood infirmity and to issues I had with the act of seeing itself. I was born with incredibly bad eyes. It was a muscular eye problem, but instead of doing traditional eye exercises, my treatment involved building things. My parents had me construct buildings of materials I found in the forest and the garden."

So he felt empowered at an early age to manipulate na-

(Opposite) Mayhew often tosses together disparate elements such as nineteenth-century cast-iron gates, a French park chair from the 1920s, and limestone blocks. The elephant ears on the left contrast with the eastern hemlock and eastern white pine.

(Right) Cast-iron gates peek out from beyond a dense planting of shrubs, including *Hydrangea paniculata*, *Cornus mas*, cotoneaster, forsythia, and *Pinus flexilis*.

23

ture and to create using natural materials. But that wasn't all. "There was also this device I had to look through that was like a stereopticon. I used it from age three to age ten. And all the pictures were of forests and natural wonders like the Grand Canyon. I just found it recently and looked through it again, and I was right back there. I said to myself, 'This is so wild. This is where a lot of my work comes from.'"

So Mayhew creates his own natural wonders. His custom-made forests always bear his stamp of spectacle. There's nothing undersized or subtle about his installations. He uses plants that are active and in your face. And he likes to sit back and watch as the plants battle for supremacy.

"I plant tight and I plant big and watch 'em fight it out," he says. "It's incredibly interesting to me to see a tree compete with another for air and light and water. When you've planted one species tight to another something magical happens. I love what hawthorns do when their branches touch and they grow together. It creates a lot of interest and adventure."

More than anything, Mayhew wants to make people think to break out of their normal way of viewing things. "I want people to wonder why you would ever put those things together. There's nothing like putting a cryptomeria next to a beech to see which one wins. You have material. You have inspiration. Put them together, and, bang, something really new is achieved. It's really important to introduce plants to each other in ways they've never met," Mayhew says. "And if one of them dies, well, the dead plant, the skeleton plant, can become a very beautiful thing too." He's not squeamish about failing. "I don't feel so bad about stuff that doesn't work. It all goes back into the pot."

Mayhew's open-air American temple is a perfectly real-

A 'Coralburst' crabapple shades a patio with its collection of potted succulents, including euphorbia, agave, and gasteria. The water garden to the left contains *Arundo donax*, *Iris kaempferi*, *Cyperus longus*, *Euphorbia palustris*, and *Typha angustifolia*.

Doug Mayhew (with Gala, his shiba inu) says he grew up in a family of tree huggers. After twenty years in the art world, he returned to his first love: the garden.

ized example of his work. In an area 35 by 15 by 25 feet, six Federal-era Corinthian columns are overrun by a weird mix of plants from bougainvillea to gourds. In anyone else's hands, these columns might seem monstrous, affected, out of place. But here they are perfectly integrated with the plantings. Mayhew has a humble 'Heavenly Blue' morning glory climbing some of the Corinthian columns, symbolically reclaiming the manufactured ruin. Others are covered with gourds. An understory of very New England *Hydrangea paniculata* rubs elbows with a Southwestern *Yucca filamentosa*. It's a scene that can't help but delight the viewer, invite investigation, and continue to surprise and please on many levels.

If you wander through the garden, eventually you'll come upon the towering Merchant's Gates. Rusted and somewhat banged up, they stand slightly ajar, leading to a scraggly lawn and an overgrown shrub and tree garden of catalpa, cotoneaster, forsythia, and yew. These plants, which normally would not work well together, are held together here by the ruin of a gate. You can't help but construct a story when you find this scene.

This type of setting symbolizes Mayhew's philosophy of what gardens and nature represent. "I think there's a garden deep inside everybody," he says. (Somehow he manages to pull off that statement without sounding sappy.) "One mission of my work is to find that garden in the heart. When I looked inside mine I found Rome and Pompeii."

Other areas of his garden are a bit more down to earth. The swimming area, though less ambitious, is certainly just as effective. A battered old glider upholstered in faded striped fabric is surrounded by odd plant combinations,

25

like a giant verbascum growing next to an Italian mermaid sculpture, and water lilies growing in an old canoe filled with water.

"I just created a very informal space on the river where you could throw on your bathing suit, grab a beer, and sit and enjoy the river. It all came together in a backhanded way."

All in all, there are four acres of surprises in these woods, providing lots of opportunity to let a childlike sense of wonder emerge. You can see how Mayhew has taken control of the property and created his own world.

"My garden is very much about getting lost," he says. "Walking through my garden, you might find yourself on a path ending at a brick wall. So you have to turn around. What does that experience do to you? I'm after that moment when your eyes open a little bit wider. That dislocation is a start. I like it when people come out and have quizzical looks on their faces. I like the fact that children are never lost in my garden, only the adults."

His choice of plant material might raise an eyebrow or two. His Connecticut garden is flush with *Colocasia*, or taro, a tropical plant that really doesn't belong here—and it won't survive the winter. But for one brief summer—my, it is something.

"I built a fern garden here, and just on a whim I ended up buying all this tropical stuff. And we planted it. Then we climbed up in trees and started hanging spider plants down through the boughs of pines. And so with just a couple of hundred tropical pieces, we wound up creating a whole new world. This Connecticut woodland suddenly was moist and wet and tropical. And it just totally changes the way you are on the land. That's what I mean when I say that gardening for me is a stream of consciousness."

Mayhew loves experimenting with new plant materials. "One time we created an entire chaparral garden indoors for one of my great patrons," he says. "They had a room where they had allowed rock ledge to come right through the floor, and they wanted mountain laurel inside. But I dissuaded them. I had something more interesting in mind.

"I built them a two-thousand-square-foot Mexican high-chaparral desert garden, where we stuck in hundreds of succulents. Working on this great arroyo desert garden gave me another jolt and another big chunk of information. I had to really learn this subject and learn it fast. That's another great thing about coming to this business from a different background."

Mayhew goes for plants that are unusual—big and active, plants that say "watch me." Plants like cryptomeria, weeping beech, climbing hydrangea. He gets infatuated. "I fall in love with my material and keep most of it. I always buy twice as much as I need. Now, all of a sudden, succulents are my favorite things. I want to stick them everywhere. Instead of accenting a vineyard with Italianate cypress, I'll just cover the whole thing in euphorbias."

He's a typical man in that he likes to move on the spur of the moment. "I always act before I think." And he likes a spectacle. He likes to make an impact, to overdo it whenever possible. "I don't like having just five purple beeches. I want to have fifteen. I don't like just twenty bareroot whatevers. I want one hundred fifty."

Mayhew is a showman. And a bit of a hustler as well. In just a few minutes he will convince you that he knows exactly what he's doing. He'll make you believe that he knows what you need and that no one else can do it for you. Most of the time he's right.

ROBERT KAUFMAN

NEW YORK AND
WILMINGTON, VERMONT

Robert Kaufman is a New York City attorney during the week, but on weekends he assumes his identity of champion Vermont vegetable grower.

YOU COULD DROP A GUY BLINDFOLDED into a certain type of man's vegetable garden, and he would feel right at home. He could hit the ground running with his hoe and start chopping weeds without damaging a single plant. That's how programmed these gardens are. He would know exactly where the rows and walkways were and precisely what was planted where. These men's gardens are nearly indistinguishable from one another.

The tomatoes are on tall stakes. The beans, earthbound, grow in rows rather than on fussy trellises. There are long rows of carrots. Cucumbers sprawl along the ground. There are no curved rows or fancy island beds. The gardens are all straight lines and square edges. And virtually the only flowers you'll see are the blossoms of the vegetables.

These classic men's gardens are nearly identical because they obey a certain logic that is obvious to almost any man. They are built around practicality, production, and routine, and they work. They are easy to weed, easy to water, easy to harvest. Sadly, because practicality rather than prettiness rules them, they are often overlooked or even scorned by the garden tastemakers.

These are the Great American Vegetable Gardens, modeled after American farms. The gardeners learned the layout and the techniques from their fathers, from USDA yearbooks, from War Department Victory Garden pam-

Kaufman's 40-by-40-foot garden is full of colorful and unusual vegetables. He grows as many as two hundred varieties a year.

phlets and bulletins. Frankly, there wasn't all that much to learn. You could find out what you needed to know by reading the back of the seed packets. Plant in straight rows one (or two) feet apart in rows three (or four) feet apart. Plant heavy. Keep like crops together. Allow plenty of room to run a rototiller between rows. Trellis the climbers or let them creep. Side-dress with 10-10-10 fertilizer twice a summer. Water when necessary. Harvest when ripe. That's it. And don't allow any flowers inside the borders, except maybe, for some mysterious reason, a long, single, funereal row of gladiolus.

All right, so the design, usually a rectangle in the back yard, is nothing spectacular. Maybe it isn't even pretty. But it's the process that counts for these gardeners. Their pleasure comes from the production. They're happy to plant the garden all at once on a single weekend in May, then spend a little time pushing a hoe or running a tiller between the rows for maybe an hour every weekend. That's about all that's required until high summer, when it's time to pick.

In their own way, these classic gardens are incredibly handsome even though they're old-fashioned. And these are the gardens that produce prize-winning tomatoes and bumper crops of peppers.

Even within the bounds of its type, though, Robert Kaufman's 40-by-40-foot garden, at his weekend home in southern Vermont, stands out. Oh, there are flower beds scattered around the wooded property, with dahlias, daylilies, phlox, and more. But those are the domain of his wife, Sheila. Bob spends all of his garden time within the confines of this rectangle.

The broad windows let a lot of light into the Kaufmans'

28

house. They also reveal the landscape outside: foundation plantings of roses and azaleas, a rolling lawn with clumps of maples and birches. And off in the distance a vegetable garden, fenced in like a fortress.

The kitchen walls are hung with antiques and old farm implements. On the table a large wooden bowl is heaped with tomatoes in fantastic colors. Purple and pink potatoes spill out of paper sacks. Beside this cornucopia is an old battered notebook. The scene tells a lot about Bob Kaufman.

As a gardener, Kaufman is a seeker, a competitor, and a record-keeper extraordinaire. He has spent twenty years searching out the best, most interesting, and intriguing vegetable varieties and recording every single bit of information about each one. As a businessman, he is a big-city lawyer. New York. Corporate law. Born in Austria, Kaufman emigrated to the United States with his parents when

he was a boy. He grew up in the city. If you had asked him where produce came from then, he would have said the greengrocer or the bodega down the street.

But in 1974 his life changed significantly when he and Sheila, a public relations executive, built a weekend house in Vermont as a winter retreat. It was the snow that attracted them, specifically the skiing. But they soon fell in love with the state in all its seasons. They loved the quiet, the beauty. There was just one problem. Back in those days it was nearly impossible to get good fresh, unusual vegetables in that part of Vermont.

But Bob Kaufman is a can-do kind of guy. If there's a problem, he knows there must be a solution. And he'll find it. If you can't buy good vegetable, then why not grow them? Never mind that he didn't know one end of a seed from the other. Never mind that he had never turned a spadeful of soil. Didn't matter. He started a little garden in

The Kaufman flower garden now occupies the spot where the vegetable garden once stood. Encroaching shade forced the food garden to a sunnier spot. All of the beds are surrounded by unobtrusive electric fences to keep out critters.

the side yard and taught himself. He read all he could in books and magazines, and started with a simple garden of tomatoes, cucumbers, beans, and lettuce in a 10-by-20-foot patch in the middle of the side lawn. Right from the start the shape conformed to the plan of the great American vegetable garden.

Bob's first crops were a success. Growing a few vegetables in a relatively benign summer climate was not as tough as corporate litigation. And though he enjoyed them more than supermarket iceberg lettuce and tasteless tomatoes, he was not fully satisfied with what he was growing. He began a quest to find the best-tasting and most productive varieties. To earn a place in his garden, a vegetable not only had to taste good and be productive, it had to look good. And if it looked a bit unusual, all the better.

Bob's obsession with odd-colored vegetables started innocently enough when he planted a package of purple-pod beans. The purple mature beans, which turn green when cooked, were unlike anything he had ever seen. He liked the idea of having something different to show his friends. He wondered if there were other odd-colored versions of the vegetables he knew. So he began searching for more unusual vegetables.

And, boy, did he find them. Now, he grows probably the greatest collection of odd, heirloom, and off-colored vegetables in Vermont, maybe in New England.

Today, in midsummer, from a distance, the Kaufman garden looks entirely conventional. It's fenced in by a five-foot-tall chicken wire fence to keep out the rabbits, woodchucks, and deer. Two rows of tomato plants on stakes run along the north side, east to west. They are always there, year after year, on the north side, just rotated a few feet each year. The rest of the rows are perpendicular to the tomatoes. There are bushy rows of carrots, peppers, potatoes, beans, and greens.

Step inside the garden, push aside the healthy foliage, and wonders appear: white carrots, white cucumbers, striped beets, purple peppers, orange-striped tomatoes, and burgundy beans. In fact, it's unusual to find a conventionally colored vegetable here. Every year this modest garden grows more than two hundred vegetable varieties from more than fifty seed companies. And this is a weekend garden, left to fend for itself during the week.

How does Bob do it? His garden is built on a masculine sense of order and control. He manages the variety of crops by reducing all the other variables as much as possible. The garden is constant, like the routine of working from nine to five, like wearing the same pinstriped suit day in and day out. The garden size, number of rows, and the number of plants in each row remain the same from year to year. And Bob doesn't fuss with succession planting during the season. He always plants the entire garden during the last two weekends of May.

The garden turns out an amazing amount of produce every year, hundreds of pounds of tomatoes and potatoes and bushel after bushel of beans and peppers. In fact, Bob can tell you exactly how much he harvests because he weighs, measures, and counts every vegetable that he picks.

When Bob began experimenting with new varieties, he quickly realized that he needed to rate them against one another in order to decide whether a variety was worth growing again. So he began tracking his harvest. Today every vegetable is weighed or counted before it makes its way to the table, and the result is recorded in a booklet. Not just every tomato and head of lettuce, but every single bean and pea pod, every carrot, cucumber, and beet.

Those records are more than just idle notes to thumb through during the long Vermont winter. They are report cards or, more accurately, performance reviews. They determine whether that variety will return the next year. Because to make it back into Kaufman's garden a variety must produce. There is no sentimentality. It's all what have you done for me lately. As in the cutthroat business world of New York, there's always someone waiting to replace you if you can't pull your weight.

In fact, in Kaufman's garden, only half of the varieties warrant a return engagement. "I'll replant the best fifty percent and replace the rest with new varieties," he says.

"Actually, I may choose either an entirely different variety or maybe the same variety but from a different grower." That's where those notebooks pay off. With them, Bob has a twenty-year baseline to measure old and new varieties against.

Over the years, there have been some consistent winners, varieties that make it back year after year. "We love the 'Green Zebras'," he says. "They're green-striped toma-

Color is the key in Kaufman's garden. He is constantly on the lookout for unusual and colorful cultivars, such as these carrots: Lobbereicher Yellow', 'Belgium White', and 'Indian Long Red'.

(Opposite) Kaufman's vegetable garden is as attractive as any flower garden in the fall, with its multicolored fruits and foliage, including this purple 'Rubine' Brussels sprouts.

Kaufman measures his success in blue ribbons from the local county fair. It's not unusual for him to take home dozens of ribbons for his unusual vegetables, such as these 'Blue Pod Capucijners' peas (above) and 'Table Gold' squash.

A MAN'S GARDEN

much more in terms of size. So I religiously pull off the suckers. It makes a big difference."

He's not unwilling to try something new, like the red plastic mulch he read about. "Last year we did half of the tomatoes on red plastic, and that half did significantly better. It really makes a difference." He can say that with confidence because he has the proof in his ledgers. Using the mulch, he harvested 25 percent more tomatoes, and they ripened 25 percent earlier.

He works about 250 pounds of manure into the garden soil every year, and the tomatoes get a little extra fertilizer. "I throw a handful of tomato food in the bottom of every one of the tomato holes," he says. The results are phenomenal. He often picks as many as 50 pounds of tomatoes per plant.

When it comes to color, other crops rival the tomatoes. There's a round white cucumber from New Zealand called 'Crystal Apple'. There's a lilac pepper that resembles an eggplant. "Some are solid purple, some have yellow stripes," he notes. 'Chiogga', the striped beet, is always a favorite. "It has red and white stripes on the inside and they don't bleed as much as red beets," Bob explains. 'Purple Viking' is his favorite potato. "Light purple with dark purple splotches, it's just gorgeous," he says.

Bob raises a wide selection of greens, including lettuce, chicory, spinach, chard, beet, and turnip greens, though he sometimes has had trouble with them. One year he had a crop failure. "I'd come back to the garden on the weekend and find that all the plants would be dried out," he says. "So I dug one out and found that something was eating the roots. I couldn't figure out what it was, but when I put out a mousetrap, I caught a vole." He grows endive for forcing. "I grow it in the garden til frost, then replant it in a sandbox in the basement to force. Then we eat endive all winter."

Even his first colored vegetable, purple-pod beans, had

toes that stay green when they're ripe." Then there's a whole school of tomatoes that masquerade as other fruits, which appeal to Kaufman for their unusual colors and textures. He lists them off: "There are lemon tomatoes. And the strawberry tomatoes. They're the shape of a strawberry and large. Don't forget orange pineapple, which is bicolored. It has a pink skin with a sort of yellow flush. The last few years I've been growing 'Black Plum' and 'Black Prince'. The latter is the tomato of choice in Siberia, where they grow them in south-facing windows. And of course there's the 'Georgia Peach', with its fuzzy skin."

In some ways Kaufman is as predictable as Heinz. Ever year he grows fifty-two varieties of tomatoes, two of each to a stake. "I prune them down to one stem," he says. "That produces a little bit less in terms of number but to compete. It has now been replaced by 'Purple Dragon', one of the varieties that was once available only through the Seed Savers Exchange. Very tasty, he says. With the renewed popularity of heirlooms, many varieties, such as 'Purple Dragon', have become available from commercial seed companies.

The harvest is as big a job as any other task in the garden year. Bob and Sheila eat very well every weekend from spring to fall. And when he returns to the city at the end of a weekend, Bob brings a bit of Vermont back with him. "I load up a couple of litigation bags with tomatoes, peppers, lettuce, and beans and bring them into the office." His coworkers look forward to Monday morning, when those vegetables are laid out for all to share. On those days Bob the provider feels especially proud of his garden.

There are many ways to measure the success of a garden. For Kaufman success is measured in numbers and colors. The reason for the garden has changed. Today, twenty-some years after he first planted a garden out of desperation, every little Vermont town has a farmer's market and an organic farm or two with fresh, crisp, colorful vegetables. Now you can buy them cheaper than you can grow them. Bob doesn't *need* to garden anymore. But for Bob it's not about cheap produce anymore. It's about the process.

For Bob Kaufman, the garden is reassuring in its sameness, even though the varieties change. Spending time in the garden is comforting and rewarding.

Also, the results are tangible. With his records he can measure his accomplishments from year to year. With his unusual varieties, he can impress his coworkers when he hauls in the harvest for all to share.

On Monday mornings he returns to work, tan from a weekend in the sun, bright-eyed from a few days working the soil and sleeping well at night, maybe with a few traces of dirt under his fingernails. What greater pleasure could a man have?

RANDALL FRIESEN

ST. CHARLES, MISSOURI

A long, curving bed of Stella d'Oro daylilies separates the lawn from the lower garden.

STANDING IN THE MIDDLE of his vegetable garden, Randall Friesen can squint just a little and imagine that he is back on the family farmette in rural Kansas. He's come a long way since then, but he has brought a lot of the farm with him.

Compared to the other yards in this upscale suburban neighborhood, Friesen's is practically a farm. The huge vegetable garden sits smack dab in the middle of the back yard. Though it has some modern touches, such as raised beds, and artistic touches, like the homemade rustic arbors, this garden does evoke an agricultural landscape. It is like a pretty, neat-as-a-pin midwestern farm. Come by at any time of the year, and you won't find a weed or a plant out of place. It looks as though a farm crew tended it day and night.

There is a lot more to this landscape than the food garden, though. Randall has roses, perennial beds, annuals, herbs, and a shade garden. But he started with vegetables,

A classic four-square herb garden occupies a corner of the back-yard vegetable patch.

(Opposite) After finishing the food gardens in the back, Randall turned his attention to the front, where he intermingled roses with junipers, cedars, and other evergreen shrubs.

which would come as no surprise to those who know him. Still, Randall himself might be hard pressed to explain why he felt the need to plant a vegetable garden even before his house was completed.

Ask a man why he gardens, why he feels compelled to push the earth around and wrestle crops from it. Chances are he will have a difficult time finding a good, logical answer. He may say that he enjoys it. He may speak of the sense of accomplishment it provides. He may mention the opportunity it offers to get out in the sun and fresh air. He may even talk about the garden as a sanctuary from work, stress, family. And vegetable gardeners will likely boast

about the money they save on produce, the fine flavor of fresh-picked vegetables. But often gardening guys can't quite put their finger on the real why. For the gardening fanatics, those who transform a landscape bit by bit, who spend hour after hour working at it, there seems to be a deeper, more compelling and mysterious reason.

If you dig deep enough, you may find that some of these men are gardening to recapture the past. Their own personal past, certainly, and on some higher level our past as a nation — our late, lamented American way of life.

Scratch a dedicated vegetable-growing man today, and you'll probably find some farming heritage in his family.

But today that kind of heritage is more and more of a rarity. It's no secret that farming has just about vanished from America. If you were born fifty years ago, the odds were good—one in seven—that you were born on a farm. Twenty years later, that chance was only one in twenty, and in 1991 fewer than one in fifty Americans were born on a farm.

However, it wasn't all that long ago that many American men grew up on a farm. And some of those sons never left home. Farms kept the family intact, with sons staying put, safe in the family. In this way they were able to experience the joy of catching up with dad, earning his respect as an adult.

Many men miss that kind of life without even realizing it, even if they never had the full experience. Such a man is Randall Friesen. It would be a stretch to say he grew up on a farm. The property was already a farm once removed or, in fifties' parlance, a "farmette," past its prime, already a statistic, and a land bargain.

"Dad bought an old farmstead in Newton, Kansas," Randall says, "three acres with a barn and silo and farmhouse built in 1909." It had been a dairy farm, but by the time Randall's dad bought it, the soil was worn out and the farm had failed. "But it gave us kids plenty of room to roam around in."

It was life on a farm—but without the chores morning, noon, and night, without the need to quit school to help the family make a living.

Instead there was a garden, a big one, which Randall's father ran efficiently. His dad had made a career in agriculture, but from behind a desk as a professor of agronomy. But he took his work home to the big garden at the old farm. The family grew enough vegetables to sell some by the road. His dad always set aside a small patch for

THE FATHER'S SON

Randall to plant a crop, "but it never turned out too well, because I didn't like to weed." Still, he learned about the soil, about plants, and about working hard with his dad. And by late summer there was always enough corn to sell door to door out of an old wagon.

Working side by side was a big part of the culture and the attraction of farming, which has always been a family affair. Farming meant that men could continue to be sons in the family. They would defer to the old man's decisions, grumble about them, for sure, but still defer.

Randall grew up and moved away, as most sons do these days. Sons (and daughters) are expected to move on, to surpass their fathers. And they do. But those who move to the suburbs and work nine to five are often left with a void. They feel a pull to return to the earth and perhaps a desire to resume a closeness with their fathers. They garden to fill that void.

Randall was no exception. He went to school, earned a medical degree, set up practice, and didn't feel dirt under his fingernails for nearly twenty years. But despite his studies and his success, the old farm of his childhood still called to him. He would visit whenever he could, and during the summer, his Dad often had some new garden project going. Randall would join him, if only for a few hours of hauling posts or digging holes.

What with medical school and residency and twenty-hour workdays, it wasn't until 1979 that he could do some planting of his own, when he and his wife bought their first home. "It was just a little house on a tiny lot in a subdivision," Randall says. "But right away I put in a small garden out back. The neighbors all thought I was crazy when I started digging up that lawn."

For four years he worked at improving the hard clay soil. It didn't take a lot of time to tend his small garden, but

A MAN'S GARDEN

(Opposite) A fruit tree allee, Randall's second major project, divided the vegetable garden in half.

Early spring reveals the bones of the vegetable garden and Randall's rustic handiwork.

that time was important to him. It made him feel settled, and he grew food for the family.

In a few years, the Friesens started looking for a bigger house. The first criterion was not the neighborhood or the school, or even the condition of the house, no, it was good soil and sun for a garden. They picked out a two-acre lot in a new subdivision.

"We were fortunate," Randall says. "It wasn't one of those subdivisions where the topsoil is long gone by the time you get there. They left the topsoil from what had been fallow farm ground. And when they put my house up, I had them pile all that topsoil aside." He was ready to plant the vegetable garden of his dreams.

Fifteen years after its creation, this suburban lot is dominated by the vegetable patch, which is in the center of the view from the deck and the kitchen window. It would be difficult to visit the Friesen house without being aware of it. At 5,400 square feet, it would seem oversized, almost farmlike, in any other neighborhood landscape, but here it's perfect. The rectangular plot is divided into six squares, separated by grassy paths with a fruit tree allee running down the center. Built on the plan of a scaled-down crop farm, it combines elements of a French parterre and a colonial kitchen garden. Each square is different. One is a formal herb garden, another hosts berries,

(text continues on page 42)

TOP TEN TOOLS FOR GUYS

One of the attractions of gardening for guys is all the neat tools.
Here are a few of our favorites.

LAWNMOWER. This is, without a doubt, the absolute number-one favorite tool of most men. It's loud, it's dangerous, it needs constant adjustment, yet it is a total no-brainer to operate. We get to spend hours every week walking behind it or, better yet, riding on it, to keep our lawn under control.

ROTARY TILLER. Remember the tiller's glory days? That was back in the sixties, when men were men and gardens were planted like mini-farms in the back yard. We wrestled those huge tillers up and down the rows. Being able to handle one was the sign of a gardening man. Raised beds rang the death knell for those behemoths and gave rise to mini-tillers. What an insult! Their ads even feature women at the handlebars. Tilling is what used to separate the boys from the girls in the garden. No more.

ELECTRIC HEDGE TRIMMER. For generations, pruning the hedge has been a man's job, even if that was the only thing he did in the garden. Watching the greenery fall before the onslaught of electric trimmers makes it even more enjoyable.

LEAF BLOWER. Talk about the rake's progress! Raking used to be a slow, meditative job. Now a guy can feel like a Star Wars storm trooper when he straps on one of those ear-splitting gasoline-powered leaf blowers.

WEED TORCH. Why bother pulling, hoeing, or even spraying weeds when you can burn 'em to a crisp with this garden-variety flame thrower?

HOE. Every guy still needs a hoe, if only to give him something to lean on as he watches the world pass by the garden. But it shouldn't be anything fancy, like a hula hoe, a motion hoe, or a collinear hoe. All it needs is an ash handle and a straight and reasonably sharp blade.

SPADE. Dig we must. That means we need a spade. But it doesn't have to be one of those fancy imported stainless-steel models that look good enough to hang over the fireplace. The $6.99 job from the local hardware store will dig just as well.

MINIATURE HAND MATTOCK. Grabbing hold of this weed-grubber, trench-digger, all-purpose chopper makes you feel like a man. This is a tool with some heft, one you wouldn't mind having in hand for a fight.

MACHETE. These are great for clearing brush. And what other excuse do you have for carrying a large knife around?

HOSE AND SPRAY NOZZLE. For lots of psychological reasons, very few gardening chores are as satisfying as standing in the yard after supper watching the sun go down and the dusk creep in as you hold a hose in your hand, spraying a soft stream of water on your garden. It's like marking your territory.

After taking a course in garden design at the Missouri Botanic Garden, Randall dug a 70-by-12-foot crescent between the house and the vegetable garden and planted the entire plot with perennials.

(Opposite) Morning glories provide summer color as they climb a rustic arbor in the vegetable garden.

(text continued from page 39)

another asparagus. Spring plantings, such as lettuce, peas, and spinach, are followed by a late crop of broccoli. Even though he has plenty of space in this garden, Randall doesn't waste it. He designs with time in mind and plants succession crops whenever possible. This garden looks right at home through all the seasons, from the spring, when bright green peas climb a fence, to summer with its potatoes, cabbages, and beans, as well as tomatoes climbing rustic homemade trellises, to fall, when the leeks grow fat and thick.

To cap off his plan, Friesen put in a trim boxwood hedge along the south side of the garden where it faces the house. That hedge now gives the garden a neat, formal look, even when he hasn't had time to pull all the weeds or strip the drying bean vines from the trellises.

Randall did not stop at the borders of the vegetable garden. Operating from an almost farmerlike approach, he decided that there would be no empty ground on this homestead. All of the land would be put to work. He felt compelled to fully develop his two acres, not leaving it fallow as lawn but making something of it.

The year after he put in the vegetable garden, he began planting the fruit trees, adding an element of permanence to the food garden. Planting them in an elegant allee allowed him an aesthetic not commonly found on midwestern farms. Randall was trying something new with those fruit trees. That willingness to take a shot at something he had never tried before came from his father. "My father is kind of an experimenter," he says. "He loves new plants, and he is always looking for unusual stuff." Even in his eighties he was experimenting with prairie plantings.

The year after planting the fruit trees, Randall dug up one corner of the vegetable garden for an herb bed. Then there was the shade garden. The iris bed. The rose garden. Eventually, a huge perennial bed. "I like to do a new garden project every year," he says.

When Randall started thinking about perennials, he knew better than to just bull ahead with shopping, digging, and planting. First he picked out the garden spot, a rectangle about seventy feet long and twelve feet wide running between the vegetable garden and the house. It was in the center of the view from the kitchen window and the deck.

But before he even stuck a spade in the sod, he decided to get some help with the design and the plants. Vegetables he knew, but ornamentals, especially perennials, were an unfamiliar to him. "The Missouri Botanic Garden has an outstanding education program," he says. "So I signed up for a class with Jim Miller." This was no one-night workshop. "It was two hours a week for eight weeks," he says. The main assignment for the class was to design a perennial garden. And Randall designed the biggest, most eye-popping bed in the class.

While he was working it out on paper, he starting doing the groundwork outdoors, too. "That fall I tilled that spot all up, so in the spring all I had to do was buy the plants and put 'em in." Randall makes it sound easy, but it wasn't. After he tilled to remove the turf, he dug the entire area—

Randall Friesen grew up working in his family's large market garden. As soon as he bought his first house, he put in a vegetable garden.

about 700 square feet—by hand. "And I worked in as much leaf mulch as I could get my hands on and about eight bales of peat moss." In the spring he was ready. "When I planted, man, the plants just took off," he says.

Now you walk through a crescent-shaped bed flush with outrageously healthy, huge plants to reach the vegetable garden. There are liatris and yarrow. "There's some miscanthus grass, *Miscanthus sinensis* 'Variegata', that's a real eye-catcher right in the center of the bed." Standing there, you might think that Randall had gone out and bought every plant mentioned in his class: day lilies, Missourie primrose, malva, purple coneflower, iris.

"It's starting to get crowded now," he admits. The plants need dividing. "I think I'll just pull everything out, redig, remulch and start all over again," he says matter-of-factly. There's something farmeresque about that attitude, that resignation to the need for hard work. In fact, he almost seems to welcome the work. On a farm, starting over each year is the name of the game. Nothing is ever finished.

That's the way it works for Randall Friesen as well. In the spring, gardening is just about a full-time job. "From April 15 to June 15, that's when I'm really busy in the garden," he says. "I'll usually spend fifteen to twenty hours a week out there. Some weeks I might spend forty hours

44

planting, pruning. I've got eighteen fruit trees and a bunch of roses, and those are always so much work."

But it's not really work in the sense of bringing home the bacon. It's more like play. The fun, the joy, the relaxation afforded by this patch of ground draw him out there. You can actually see the tension leave him when he steps off the deck and crosses the lawn to the vegetable garden. "My wife used to call this garden my two-acre nerve pill," Friesen says.

But let's not forget the harvest, which was the genesis. That's what this little faux farm was all about when he started. "There's some great food that comes out of this garden. There's nothing like being able to go out to the garden and pick it fresh," he says. "There's no restaurant in the world that can give me food like that."

Then there's the physical aspect. "Just working in the soil, rather than sitting in front of the TV, gives me a lot of pleasure. Seeing the fruits of my labor gives me some meaning and some worth. When I can see very real results from my labor, that gives me a lot of satisfaction."

In a way, the garden defines him, much the way a person growing up on a farm is defined as a farmer.

"Around here people know me as a gardener," Randall says. "I've been in the local paper with my garden. I'm the only guy around here who gardens."

But for all the reasons that Randall loves to garden, the primary one may be the joy of working with familiar plants, working in harmony with the seasons, doing what he's done and his father has done for decades.

Even after all these years, the garden still connects him with his father. His latest project was building a ninety-foot-long rustic cedar arbor with his dad, now in his eight-

ies. They built it together over the course of a week. Digging holes, hauling and stripping logs, teasing each other, working together. Randall talks about how it was modeled after Tottenham, about how it's going to look when it's covered with roses and morning glories. His face brightens and his voice lightens when he talks about the building of it, working side by side with his dad. "Man, that was fun! It was just one of those neat experiences you never forget."

In the past, once a year he and his wife would celebrate the garden together. They'd invite as many as forty friends over for a garden party a harvest feast. He provided the ingredients, and she, a wonderful cook, made a lovely dinner from them.

They set up tables on the lawn beside the garden, and ate and drank and laughed well into the night until the mosquitoes chased them indoors. Randall never enjoyed his garden more. It was like laying out his history and his family and himself for his friends and guests as reflected in the garden that they were enjoying. It was at those times that he shared his gardening most with his wife.

The parties ended after his wife died unexpectedly in the mid 1990s. "I do find some solace here," Randall explains. "The years since my wife died have been really tough. But gardening relieves some of that tension. I wrote to my father and said, I'm really glad that you taught me gardening. It has been beneficial to me over these trying years.

"I know I've made all kinds of mistakes out there," he says. "But it doesn't really bother me. The fun comes from knowing that every single plant out here was one that I put in myself. The fun comes from watching things grow and watching the landscape change every year."

Howard Dill won the world record for the largest pumpkin in 1980 and went on to break the record three more times.

THE PUMPKIN KING

HOWARD DILL

WINDSOR, NOVA SCOTIA

SOMETHING ABOUT PUMPKINS wants to be big. And some men just want to make them grow bigger. They want to grow a pumpkin that can't be lifted by a single man, a pumpkin that makes people's jaws drop, a pumpkin visible from the road. And they've gotten their wish. Over the past thirty years, growing giant pumpkins has become a highly competitive sport as the technology has blossomed. Pumpkins are growing bigger than anyone could have dreamed just ten years ago and records are being smashed like squash dropped from a helicopter.

As in many great revolutions, there's one man behind the action. That man is Nova Scotian Howard Dill. He is the Babe Ruth or, perhaps more appropriately, the Gordie Howe of giant pumpkin growing. Now in his sixties, Dill, tall and lanky, sports a dark tan on his craggy face. His chore clothes are a battered baseball cap, a pair of old, shiny Wrangler jeans, and a black-and-red wool shirt. He's

got that Jimmy Stewart aw-shucks look. Or he might remind you of Ray Bolger in *The Wizard of Oz*, while he was still a farmhand.

Like many Canadians, Howard Dill was a rabid hockey fan growing up on the farm. He loved the speed, the physicality, the competition. (In fact, he claims that the sport of hockey was first played on a pond on the Dill farm in Windsor.) For him, though, farm chores came first. "We had all cows on the farm," Dill says. "I learned how to milk a cow at a very young age. Because of all the chores, I didn't have time to play the game like the rest of the boys." So instead of playing hockey, he did the next best thing and became a collector of hockey memorabilia. Dill now has one of the largest private collections in Canada.

That satisfied some of his sports urge. But he still had a

Atlantic Giant®
World's Largest Pumpkin

HOWARD DILL WITH HIS 1999, 875 POUND PUMPKIN.

7 SEEDS
PACKED FOR
2001

Dill's Atlantic Giant^{PVP}
Unauthorized Propagation Prohibited—PVP No. 8500204
Photo: Sherman Hines

Howard Dill decided to share
his success with the pumpkin-
growing world, so he founded a
seed company, Howard Dill
Enterprises, to sell his Atlantic
Giant pumpkin seeds.

competitive itch that went unscratched until he discovered pumpkins. If you think about it, you will realize that pumpkins are one of the few crops grown primarily for amusement. Oh, sure, thousands of acres are grown for pie filling (though much of the canned pumpkin is in reality hubbard squash), but that's not why we gardening men grow them. We grow them as ornaments. We grow them because they're big and heavy. Forget those new ones— they're more gourds than anything. When it comes to pumpkins, the bigger, the better. So why not see how big we can make those suckers grow: a hundred pounds? two hundred pounds? How about half a ton?

And thus the sport of giant pumpkin growing was born. For years, though, the competition languished. Champions routinely weighed in at around four hundred pounds. Someday, the growers dreamed, there will be a five-hundred-pound pumpkin. Someday, a pumpkin-growing hero will come along to take the sport to the next level, to give it 110 percent, to grow one for the Gipper. That hero turned out to be Howard Dill.

To a farmer, the equivalent of hockey's Stanley Cup is a blue ribbon at the local county fair. In that regard, Howard's father was a hero. His prize crop was (what else?) pumpkins. "My dad was very proud of his garden. Besides the farm, he always had his own vegetable patch, where he grew crops for the local fall fair," Dill says. He still fondly recalls the excitement of preparing the entries, the anticipation of waiting for the weigh-in and the ribbons to be awarded, the comparison with other entries. The competition lifted life beyond the humdrum, beyond the milking and the chores that had to be performed every day. This was something different, something special.

To the young Howard, those seventy-five- to eighty-pound pumpkins seemed huge. But he started daydreaming and scheming. "I thought, 'Wouldn't it be nice it if you could grow something even bigger.' Those pumpkins on

HOWARD DILL ON

☛ Do a soil pH test and add lime or sulfur as necessary to bring the pH to 6.5–7.

☛ Add lots of organic matter to the soil.

☛ Sow the seeds twenty-five to thirty feet apart in each direction.

☛ As the plants grow, thin the young pumpkins to no more than one per vine and no more than two per plant.

☛ Apply a water-soluble liquid fertilizer every week. For the first month use a fertilizer that's high in phosphorus, then switch to one that's high in potassium after the fruit forms.

☛ Water when necessary, but don't overwater. Dust for insects as necessary.

☛ Grow until frost or until vines die.

Windsor, Nova Scotia
"Where the Pumpkin is King"

"This is BIG PUMPKIN Country"

Dill has attracted national attention to the small town of Windsor, Nova Scotia, now known as the giant pumpkin mecca.

display at the county fair all had different characteristics, and I thought that if you could combine all those traits you'd have a giant."

So rather than make his mark on the ice, he dug into the pumpkin patch. He started from ground zero and taught himself breeding—and that was a big part of the satisfaction. "I didn't have any college education," he says. "I had to teach myself the genetic part of it. At first I didn't really know what I was doing. I just knew that I had to make selective crossings of the biggest and best, male and female, and hope for the best."

His technique worked. Imagine the excitement and anticipation he felt. You plant a seed, wait months in the uncertain Nova Scotian climate for a fruit to form. You watch it put on weight in a race against the first frost. Then finally the harvest, when you find that your seat-of-the-pants breeding has paid off with a pumpkin noticeably bigger than the previous year's. Imagine the pride that comes from knowing you've actually created something new, bigger, better—on your own.

Dill describes the process. "Over the years I would see growth by one hundred or two hundred pounds per generation, and after a while I said to myself, 'I believe I'm for real.' There was always a doubt that it might be a flash in the pan."

He started his quest for the great pumpkin in the 1960s, and by the late 1970s he was ready to stand toe to toe with the big boys. In 1979 he came out of nowhere and won the world championship with a 459-pound pumpkin. Some of the regulars on the pumpkin circuit were not impressed, though. "They thought I was a fluke," Dill snorts. But he came back and won it the next year. And the year after that. By then he was a legend.

The following year, 1982, he lost the crown by a mere five pounds. He didn't sulk, though. He just kept at it. At that time the holy grail was the five-hundred-pound pumpkin. "That would be like running a four-minute mile," Dill says. Some predicted it couldn't be done, but Dill had no doubts. He had seen the weight of the winners increase by fifty, sixty, seventy pounds a year and knew they hadn't reached their limit yet. So he kept breeding. He kept growing bigger pumpkins and crossing them with each other, and he began offering his seeds for sale. All the while he kept careful records, and as others grew champions from his seeds, the accolades poured in from across Canada and the United States and around the world.

By the 1980s, whenever people talked of giant pumpkins, they talked of Howard Dill. With his seeds, the five hundred-pound barrier was smashed, and the pumpkins just kept getting bigger and bigger. In 1998 the thousand-pound barrier was broken.

Dill became a celebrity. "I seemed to grow into it. I never could have imagined . . . If anybody told me I would be selling seed in Russia, I'd have told him he was crazy. But we do. We sell seed packets in seventeen different languages. We have a twenty-acre farm in California where we grow the seed." But success hasn't changed him. Yes, he has a small seed company to sell his Atlantic Giant pumpkins, but he still works the farm, still milks the cows twice a day. And if you stop by, he'll find the time to talk pumpkins—or hockey—with you. He'll show you the pond, drag out his collection of autographed hockey sticks. "I'm proud to say I'm still the same," he says. "If you came here into the yard, you might find me in my old clothes. I'd say 'Yep, I'm Howard.' I never got swell-headed. I met an awful lot of good people, I'll tell you that. It's great just to see the fun that other people get out of it.

"The thing I find most amazing is the number of people who get hooked on giant pumpkin growing after they retire," Dill says. "People write and say, 'I'm eighty-five years old and I'd like to know how I can grow a bigger one next year.' It just seems to give them something to look forward to."

Dill claims that giant pumpkin growing is the fastest-growing sport hobby in the world. And though it's competitive, it's a joyous sport. "Look," he says, "the thing that impresses folks most about these pumpkins is the size. And the bigger they are, the happier people seem to be."

Felder's irreverent interpretation
of the traditional picket fence
incorporates dangerous-looking
spikes and upended bottles.
The red rose was grown
from a cutting of an old
cemetery variety.

FELDER RUSHING

JACKSON, MISSISSIPPI

Zoe Rushing studies the front-yard concrete walkway embedded with trinkets, such as Mardi Gras doubloons and marbles found in the garden. Felder created the walk to make life easier for his whistling mailman.

THERE IS NO OTHER FRONT YARD in Jackson quite like Felder Rushing's, that's for sure. In fact, there may be no yard like it in all of America. When people stumble upon this place, they shake their heads in wonder and amusement the way folks do when they see the Watts Towers for the first time. It is, in its own way, another roadside attraction.

This small front yard is Felder Rushing's playground. The first thing that catches your eye may be the bottle tree, a dozen or so blue bottles—bluer than the bluest spruce—sticking out from a pole like glinting glass boughs. Or it may be the leaning tower of tires, all painted an institutional green, that threatens to topple into the plants below. And what's covering the rusted I-beams standing straight up in the center of the garden? Refrigerator magnets. "Industrial-strength refrigerator magnets," Felder points out.

There's no question that the person behind this garden is a man—or possibly a kid disguised as a man. That's Felder, long curly hair tumbling out from under a battered 'dozer cap, shirttails hanging out of his baggy jeans. With his ever-present twinkle and grin, he looks like a chunky gnome.

Felder fools people. When they see him climbing out of his beat-up pickup truck and hear the twang in his voice, some might dismiss him as a lightweight, even a clown.

He won't mind letting them think that for a while, as he gradually reveals the true depth of his character and knowledge. There is a lot more to Felder than meets the eye or the ear. He earned a master's degree from Mississippi State University. He writes a weekly state-wide newspaper column, hosts a call-in show on twenty-four radio stations, and appears weekly on public television. A Mississippi state cooperative extension agent for twenty years, he's one of the first people Mississipians turn to for expert garden advice.

That "aw, shucks" attitude is part of the schtick that makes this eighth-generation Mississipian one of the most sought-after speakers on the garden circuit. Felder delights the ladies of local garden clubs as well as the hard-to-impress hort professionals. Whether he's speaking at the local hardware store or the tony Colonial Williamsburg Garden Symposium, Felder wows 'em. He has charm, but he also knows plants and gardening techniques.

Felder has written or cowritten five books, including the award-winning and totally enjoyable *Pass-Along Plants*. He's a damn good writer—good enough so that some of his work appears in the anthology *Writers in the Garden*. Ironically, in the books on tape version, Felder's piece is read by an actor with an upper-class British accent. One reviewer complained, "Everybody knows Felder is a redneck." Everybody *thinks* they know that, and that's fine with him.

For Felder Rushing, gardening is an activity akin to sneaking out of the house while Mom's not looking and playing in the dirt. Gardening reawakens the little boy in him. "Working" in the yard is like lazing through a long summer day when every bug has to be investigated close up, when this stick needs to be nailed to that box. And the

garden is the place where holes have to be dug and water poured into them. Why? Just to see what happens. Just because it's fun.

You probably wouldn't find this kind of chaos, the whimsical, unchecked prankish urges in a woman's garden. For better or worse, for whatever reason, it is usually men who are the fun-lovers, the silly-doers. And in this

man's garden there's something that wants to cause a little fuss and get a little attention, and to see how much he can get away with.

In this case he gets away with plenty. Felder's wife, Terryl, an attorney and accountant, allows Felder his front-yard rebellion though she did raise a stink when he built a bathtub shrine to his grandmother's chicken in the middle of the front yard. "She's upset about my new grotto," Felder admits. "I took my great-grandmother's bathtub and stood it on end rather than throw it away. Then I drilled holes in the rim and attached antique glass doorknobs. Then I hung a spotlight and shined it on my grandmother's concrete chicken smack in the middle of the tub.

"My wife doesn't want people to think that I'm poking fun at Catholics," Felder says. "But I wasn't trying to make an irreverent statement. I was just trying to create a place of high esteem for my grandmother's chicken." He says that he'll eventually move it to a less obvious location.

Felder calls himself a motley fool, a court jester. Like that jester, he possesses an uncommon wisdom, and he's happy to share it, usually by hitting you over the head with it. Once you get over the shock and look past the "junk," this landscape helps you remember what gardening is meant to be. There's the joy that we felt as kids when we first saw a caterpillar crawling up a milkweed pod. There's the surprise we enjoyed when a flower bloomed overnight or when we tasted the first juicy, ripe tomato.

This garden is, first and foremost, a place to relax in while surrounded by plants. There are plenty of plants—more than 450 species in this small urban yard. Felder has blooms all year round, from evergreen camellias in February to roses such as 'Aloha' and 'Martha Gonzalez' in late fall. At first glance you might conclude that this garden has been thrown together willy-nilly. But that's not the case.

(Opposite) Zoe and Ira hunt for tadpoles in one of the small water features. Felder dug up the front walk to install the little pond.

Felder's front yard used to be all lawn and wide open to the street. The lawn is gone, and now a winding path is bordered by heat-loving plants such as sanvitalia.

Felder knew that in order to accomplish everything he wanted, to fit in all the plants he wanted as well as all the stuff, he'd have to have a plan, for even a yard that looks spontaneous has to have some underlying structure. And even though he has a master's degree in horticulture, he looked to others for help.

"I sought some advice from a lot of designer friends, but I settled on Rick Griffin, a local landscape architect. He gave me a pattern that instantly worked. I just had to do a little bit of fine-tuning," Felder says. He explains that there's sound architecture behind Griffin's designs. "He can take a small space and carve it up into several smaller but more usable spaces."

That was the perfect approach for this lot, which isn't even sixty feet across. "Three people couldn't park their cars in the street in front of my yard," Felder says. But there's plenty going on in that little bit of space. Along with all the plants, there are thirty pieces of yard art. He and Terryl and their two kids, Ira and Zoe, spend a lot of time there. "We spend more time in my front yard in a week than the neighbors do in their yards in a year," he says. "That's cuz all they're doin' is mowin'. We're sittin' and talkin' and watchin' and feelin'. It's plenty big enough to satisfy my need to have lots of thotchkes: little unusual plants, little detailed things—and a lot of yard art."

Some of that art serves a purpose, besides amusing Felder and shocking the neighbors. For example, he was confronted by an eyesore in his front yard (some would say he still is, but at least these are *his* eyesores). "Right in the middle of the yard was a telephone pole that serviced five houses," he says. "It couldn't be moved, but I figured that maybe it could be disguised. So I asked Rick for some ideas. He had me put up a bunch of cedar poles the same color and texture as the telephone pole. Then we strung concrete reinforcing wire between them to make a trellis, and, by God, that made the telephone wires and pole dis-

appear." Even though it worked, Felder made some changes. "I eventually replaced the trellis with I-beams. Got six of 'em all covered with refrigerator magnets. There's my travel history right there. I've got forty-two states. Some guys collect orchids, I collect refrigerator magnets."

But what about the plants, Felder? "It looks like a mish-mash," he admits, "but everything is there for a reason. I embrace a cottage-style garden, as opposed to the subur-

56

(Opposite) By fall the helianthus, aster, and eupatorium are bursting out of their britches in the front yard. The jack-o'-lantern was made from an old tire.

(Above) A greenhouse, built onto the back of a garage-turned-play-room, hosts tender plants in winter. It's also a great place to start seeds. The shady back yard is home to a collection of potted plants.

ban style. In the suburban style, you design and plant it all at once. Then you try to keep it at that level by arresting the development of the plants through mowing and pruning." In fact, Felder suggests, perhaps with his tongue lodged in his cheek, there may be more gardening skill involved in maintaining the suburban style: pruning, keeping the edges neat, controlling weeds. He can't resist talking about his unique method of edging his plantings— with a model train. Yes, there is a train running through

Some might call it trash. Felder calls it cheap art. Here's his re-cycled-tire Christmas tree, which is sometimes decorated with hubcap ornaments. Stand-ing tall in the front yard, it's per-fectly visible from the street.

Felder's garden, but somehow it doesn't have the same fastidious feeling as those of the railroad garden guys.

"I've got an electric train that snakes around the perimeter of the open spaces," Felder says. "Some people line their beds with rocks. Mine are lined with track. Instead of having monkey grass around the edge, I've got a train. It's like having grass that circles at five miles an hour." As it travels around, it clips off the weeds that trail over the tracks. "That's what I use for my edging material," he says. "It keeps the bed nice and neat." And, he adds, he can use it to deliver a bottle of beer to someone sitting on the deck.

Sooner or later he always gets back to the subject of style. "In the suburban style, there's a lot more attention to detail and pride in workmanship. A lot of guys like to mow grass and prune because it shows they've done something. Men's gardens tend to take that to extreme. We try to make our lawn greener than the guy's down the street. A lot of it has to do with controlling your perimeters. You can make your mark by having a neater, greener lawn."

Not Felder. He doesn't need grass to measure his manhood. Even though he is the state extension turf specialist, there's not a square inch of lawn in his yard. "Terryl would rather we had a bit of grass to mow," he says. He does admit that a patch of turf performs important functions in a landscape, but he has lawn substitutes that do the same.

"A lot of folks have lawns to keep things neat, or to provide a flat space, a void, to set off other plants. I can do that with mulch. On the other hand, if you don't have a lawn, you don't have a place for birds to swoop. But my decks serve that purpose. My decks are not cluttered. Neither are my water gardens. I don't grow any plants in my

Of all the "vernacular art" on his property, bottle trees are Felder's favorites. He has seven of them in his small yard.

59

Felder's grandmother's concrete chicken has been afforded a place of honor in a bathtub shrine beyond an arch in the front yard. Felder believes that every garden should have a portal.

water gardens—two in-ground ponds and a cooking kettle full of water. I need that flat open surface that the water provides.

He's tried to picture himself in a standard American landscape. "If I had a suburban-style garden, it would be the most anal-retentive," he says. "Why? Because I'm a guy. A woman wouldn't fuss so much with the weeds. She wouldn't prune the shrubs so severely." But, he points out, "a woman wouldn't have a train running through the front yard either."

He says his father did the suburban thing—trying to grow grass in a yard that was constantly under attack by kids and dogs. "It was partly a control thing for him. But it was also a result of being hounded to keep the yard looking nice, to keep the grass thick and the dirt down so the kids wouldn't track it into the house." His mother was a southern garden-club lady who loved African violets. "She had three books of blue ribbons from flower shows," Felder says. "From her I was exposed to the pride part and the stickin'-with-it part of gardening."

But his real gardening influence was his great-grandmother. "She grew hundreds of daffodils and beaucoup other plants. She was into wildflowers long before it was acceptable. She had a bird sanctuary. In short, she was a rebel in the garden." That sounds familiar.

"One of my first gardening memories was of her showing me a beautiful caterpillar on a black-eyed Susan," he says. "And she didn't say 'bad bug.' On the contrary, she told me it was okay."

He learned an important lesson from his mother and his great-grandmother. "Watching women grow old in their gardens, reaching a sort of a plateau where they basically feel that they have earned the right to be doing what they pleased in their yards, I said to myself, 'I'm not gonna wait till I'm an old woman to start enjoying my garden.'"

There's no doubt he does enjoy it. "Terryl doesn't mind it too much," he says. "She knows that it's harmless. It's my version of hangin' out in a bar. So she thinks of my garden as being like some men's bass boats. It's my obsession and my toy. It's my vehicle for flying away. And she's figured it out."

If you take away the train and the bottle tree and all the toys, you come to the heart of Felder's garden: the plants. Tough, hardy plants that work hard year-round. "When I'm in the garden, I'm surrounded by lots of flowers and trees and textures and scents," Felder says. "Every day of the year I've got something blooming. Every week there's something fragrant. I use all four corners of my garden. I've got more than four hundred species in an area as big

Felder can turn an ordinary tire into an extraordinary planter in about seven minutes. The tires provide the round part of his formula for good landscape design: "something spiky, something frilly, and something roundy."

The Rushings' cluttered cottage garden runs right to the street from the front porch, where a found rose from Texas grows up a homemade privacy screen.

as some people's carports." Felder calls it riotous. His mother says it resembles "a kaleidoscope having a stroke."

This garden is a place for experimenting and playing hunches. "In my little garden, I've got high areas and dry areas and all kinds of microclimates. When I see really good accidental wildflower combinations on the roadside, I try to copy it here," he says. "When I dug my little water garden in the front yard, I piled up the clay and left it there in a berm. I figured that after I'm gone, somebody's gonna want to fill that hole back in. Might as well leave the dirt there for them. So I saved the dirt, but it's a pile of clay. Then I started thinking: what grows better in clay than sumac? Nothin'. In good dirt it gets invasive and its color is not as bright. Now when somebody says nothin' will grow in clay I show them my sumac."

He really doesn't want more space. "By keeping it small and tight I force myself into making choices. The size of the garden is like a governor on my desires. For example, I've only got spots for three daylilies in my yard. So if I want a new daylily, well it's gonna have to be good enough to replace one that's already there.

Felder's the first to admit that his garden is not classical. "If you were to plop my garden down in Europe, it would look trashy," he says. "But I do know about horticulture and design. I do have standards in my head. It's just that my garden doesn't measure up to them. It doesn't have to! As an extension agent, I'm expected to have certain standards, to show a certain amount of finesse. But this garden is partly a way for me to get away from that. When I walk into my guarded area (and that's what a garden is, a guarded area), when I come in here I'm away from my clients. I don't have to rake the leaves. I don't have to have the latest annuals, or meatball- or gumdrop-shaped plants. I don't have to prove anything. You might say this is my way of unsnapping that too-tight horticultural brassiere."

Of course, gardening folks know who he is and where he lives. They read his newspaper column, and they drive by to take a look at what he's up to. "Sometimes there's a constant parade of people coming by, cars bumper to bumper," he says. But they can't really see the garden from the street, even though most of it is in the front yard. "My garden is designed from the house looking outward," he says. "When people drive by all they see is the back of it.

"They can't even imagine what's here," he says. "If they took five steps into my garden they would be amazed. After five steps in you have to make a left-hand turn; make that turn, and you're in a different world. I've protected my perimeters. We can sit on the front deck half-nekked, with a big fire going, and they can't see or hear none of it from the sidewalk. But I didn't put my main garden out in the front to make any kind of statement. It's in front because the front faces south.

There is a method to his plant madness: this is not just a random collection. "To make the cut, the plants have to grow in bad, poorly prepared soil. They gotta withstand absolute utter neglect—no pesticides, no irrigation. Last summer I didn't water a single in-the-ground plant, and we had a major drought," he says proudly. The potted plants provide just enough watering relaxation. "Watering is a therapy for me, it's my mowing the grass. I cut my hose off to exactly long enough so that I can water the farthest plant from the faucet so I wouldn't have to deal with excess hose. I was told that nothing does well here in summer," Felder says. But again he's proven the experts wrong. "I've found plants that just keep blooming in the heat of the South."

His garden is designed so that it doesn't require a lot of fussing. "These days I spend a total of about fifteen to twenty minutes a month on actual garden maintenance," Felder says. "Mostly it's just little routine stuff. When I'm walking out to the mailbox to get the paper, maybe I'll do a little weeding on the way. I find a weed, I pull it out and drop it behind something to let it compost in place. It's more like a den that needs to be picked up than a living room that's kept spic and span for company."

Everything he does has a sound horticultural basis—well, almost everything. He was surprised by the view expressed when he first started taking horticulture classes. "I've never forgotten the first time a professor told me a plant is not worth anything till somebody gives you a penny for it." Felder was shocked. "But from his standpoint, from his masculine paradigm, he was absolutely right." And that's not an untypical attitude for a lot of men. "Women tend to garden for the love of it," Felder notes. "Men tend to garden for control. If they get into the horticultural business, it's for economic reasons, trying to profit from what they do."

THE MASCULINE
QUEST FOR FIRE

We men are fascinated by fire. Why do you think we love to barbecue? It's not for the food, it's because we get to play with fire. In fact, there's nothing like the alpha waves produced by gazing at flickering flames to bring out the primal guy. Felder Rushing has a fire pit in his front yard, and he's spent hours staring into the light, finding insight and inspiration. He believes that our need to cling to and click a TV remote control is emotionally akin to stirring a fire with a metal poker.

Felder says it's easy to make a fire pit. "All you need is a safe place that's far enough from flammable materials (look up!) in case something hot pops out," he says. "Watch out for rolling logs." For practical reasons, you should surround the pit with bricks or rocks, or you could use the cut-off end of a defunct propane tank like those you see next to farmhouses. "Anything that'll hold burning stuff without burning itself will do," Felder says.

"For a long time, I had my metal tub set on bricks, to get it far enough above the wooden deck to prevent scorching. Later I got a friend to weld handles on the sides, and also three railroad spikes on the bottom as legs. I cover it during rainy weather, and empty the ashes from time to time, and that's all there is to maintenance."

Most municipalities that allow fire pots will let you have an open fire pit as long as you use it for recreation—"not for getting rid of old tires," Felder scolds. "Check with the fire marshal just in case, or be cool about it—no huge bonfires. And burn pizza boxes just one at a time. They flame up really big, and rise and float above the fire like blinking space ships—and no one knows where they'll land!"

Felder Rushing, state extension service agent, author, and self-proclaimed motley fool, plays with one of his garden toys.

He draws an analogy with cooking. "Most chefs are men," he notes, "but most cooks are women. Women cook for survival. They cook because they need to. But men become chefs to get accolades."

That's clearly not Felder's reason for gardening. Joy and wonder are the profits of his plantings. If you stop for a visit, he'll start the train and let you run it for a while. He'll light a fire in the fire pit and poke at it for a spell with his homemade poker. His is a garden where there's lots to do and touch and play with, like a discovery garden for adults. "I love the tactile. We've got a big old hairy rope on the front porch, and you can't get to our door without touching it. Kids love to swing on it. When people leave through our front door, for just an instant you see in their eyes the thought that they could swing on this thing. Maybe they never would, but they realize they *could*."

Felder does see his garden as making a contribution to the greater good by setting an example for gardening men. "I'm spreading a larger legacy, that yard art is not only okay but fun, too. That you can combine tough plants and garden whimsy. We men may not wear earrings, but we can put flamingos in the front yard. Or we can put up I-beams and cover them with refrigerator magnets. And what better way to celebrate your history?"

For some men, gardening is an excuse to use loud, dangerous power tools. Not for Felder. He owns only one power tool, and it's not a lawn mower. "The most macho tool I have is a leaf blower," he says. "I can herd leaves around like you wouldn't believe. Other than that I do everything with the very best hand tools."

Like Felco pruners. "They're simple, straightforward, with no gadgets." Like something called an English ladies' turning fork. Now that could not be less macho, but it works. It's small. It's well balanced. "Last time I was in England, I bought one, and the clerk said: 'But that's a ladies' fork.' And I said, 'Get past the name, man, it works.' It's like that deodorant ad—made for a woman, but strong enough for a man.

"But my very favorite tool is a sort of pint-sized pickax with a pick and a cutting blade," he says. "You can handle it with one hand, but that thing will crack open the hardest clay. I can grab stuff with one hand and whomp stuff with the other."

That reminds him of a good rule of thumb: "Don't even try anything you can't do while holding a beer in one hand."

ROBERT KOURIK

OCCIDENTAL, CALIFORNIA

Robert Kourik digs worms! He doesn't till his garden but instead loads it with mulch, and worms thrive in the rich soil.

To FIND ROBERT KOURIK, you drive up a half-mile-long winding gravel driveway through thick brush and second-growth redwood trees to the top of a 1,200-foot mountain. Keep an eye out for foxes and bobcats along the way.

At the end of the driveway, park and walk up the wood-chip path to the house, where Robert—sandy hair retreating from his forehead, short beard almost always framing a smile—will greet you. He'll probably be ready with a joke or a guffaw.

Robert Kourik, landscape designer and author, an expert on irrigation, gray water, and lavender, will excuse you if you don't notice the plantings at first. In fact, he would be disappointed if you weren't initially distracted by all the other stuff.

What stuff? Wire cages festooned with favorite pieces of used clothing, broken clay pots, and other personal artifacts. Ceramic slabs hanging from trees, looking like gravestones or phallic symbols, depending on your point of view. There are what Robert calls "stairways to heaven." Scattered around the grounds are more broken clay pots, bamboo chicken cages, blue glass floats. The outdoor office has its own visual horticultural puns. An old wooden desk has plants growing out of its open drawers, and on top, thyme creeps out of the floppy-drive bay of an old Kaypro computer. Why that herb? "That's how you judge the efficiency of a computer," Robert says. "By its access thyme." An old phone hangs on the wall of the house. Chunks of obsidian sit on the desktop, and some

Will work for food . . . Robert unearths a batch of bean-hole beans for a barbecue.

67

(Left) A heavy wire cage that protects an Italian cypress becomes a work of art when adorned with clay pots and shards. Robert calls it the stairway to heaven.

(Opposite) Robert's outdoor world revolves around his barbecue. A cast-iron pot full of beans is buried beneath coals topped with sand decorated in a nautilus motif.

thirty pages of a manuscript slowly turning into papier-mâché in the weather.

There are bones everywhere. "I have a lot of bones in my landscape. I'm constantly collecting them. I've got a ton of sheep skulls from my neighbor's place. He was a sheep farmer, and not a very good one." A ribbon crowns a plant cage, "symbolizing all that's left after I finish writing a book," Robert says. A trail of bones leads to a clearing beside the house. That's the barbecue area, the center of this man's universe. There's a fire pit, a bean hole, and piles of bones and skulls arranged in what Kourik calls constructed archeology. A large slate slab is held up by flue tiles. Three disks from a farm harrow, balanced on more flue tiles, hold barbecue tools and sauces. For the rustic comfort of the guests, there are chairs carved out of tree trunks and covered with moss.

This is the ultimate guy place. The entire landscape appears to be built around the barbecue pit. But this is not your suburban deck with a gas-fired grill. This is outdoor cooking a la Piggy in *The Lord of the Flies*. As you sit on a stump, you can hear water trickling from a little waterfall that spills out from under native huckleberry. This place is reminiscent of a clearing in the woods where little boys go to read comic books, eat candy bars, and drink soda pop from glass bottles.

Kourik says that this is truly a man's territory. "Over the eons, as we evolved, women lost the capacity to do barbecues. The twenty-fourth gene on the forty-second chromosome give guys sole territory of barbecue."

Most women don't have a lot of skulls lying around in their gardens either. "It's funny," he says. "Women are generally the ones who say my constructed archeology is morbid. They say I'm fascinated with death, but I remind them of Georgia O'Keeffe, an inspiration of mine. And besides, that's what gardening is about. At least fifty percent of any garden is evolving toward death. Entropy will win out."

Resignation and acceptance of the inevitable echo through this garden. Because if entropy doesn't win out, nature, drought, weeds, or the deer will. Kourik is constantly working around the deer. So he protects a few specimen plants, like the chartreuse elderberry, with cages and prunes his fruit trees so the deer can't reach the fruit.

This is the most natural sort of gardening. Kourik doesn't rail against and resist the limitations, he goes with the flow. He has chosen not to defy or defeat the climate, the rain, the clay soil, and especially the deer, but to coexist with them. That attitude is what makes his garden one of the most remarkable natural plantings, though it's not exclusively native, for it has its share of exotics.

After you've checked out all of the whimsical features, and your eyes adjust, the way they do when you walk from a dark room into the sunlight, you're finally ready to ap-

In what Robert calls "constructed archeology," he arranges bones and pottery shards around his property. Here they adorn his homemade slate and brick barbecue.

preciate the plantings. At first you don't so much see the garden, as you smell it. It's not an overpowering scent that twitches your nose. It's a subtle background aroma of herbs: rosemary, lavender, santolina. In time you realize the air is thick with fragrance. When you look for the source, you see large patches of vertical rosemary on one side of the house. On the other side of the path are patches of a weeping rosemary, along with a rare pine-scented variety.

When he moved to northern California with the hippie migration of the seventies, Kourik may have thought he was coming to a gardening paradise. But now, years later, sitting on his mountaintop in Occidental, he knows that this is not an easy place to garden. He doesn't pretend it is. He doesn't beat his head against the garden wall. Instead, he hatches schemes that allows him to garden easily and in harmony with this place.

Of his techniques, he says: "I call it inspired laziness. I average less than two hours a week maintaining my two thousand square feet." He spends more time mowing the meadow in summer to keep the fire danger down than he does working on his landscape.

The garden is easy because it is all no-till. Kourik rarely sticks a spade into the soil these days, and he doesn't pamper the plants with water or fertilizer. When he plants a fruit tree, for example, he puts it on a drip system using gray water collected from his shower for a year or two. After that it has to fend for itself. "Many of them have been on their own for fifteen years, and they produce more fruit because of it," he says.

He does have to protect the trees from deer, though, or he would have no fruit. Instead of using elaborate fences or cages, he simply prunes carefully. Yes, his dozen or so fruit trees—apples, Asian pears, and a rare Burbank plumcot—are odd looking. It's not only because different varieties are grafted onto one tree. It's their shape. "I prune them so that the first branch is at least six feet off the ground, so the deer can't reach them," Kourik says. "Then I keep the top pruned back to ten feet so I can harvest easily."

Because of the deer Kourik cannot grow tomatoes, lettuce, most of the usual vegetables. "A lot of people don't consider this a food garden because of the deer," Kourik says. "But I consider it a food garden because of the fruit, and because I cook and do all sorts of things with lavender and other herbs the deer won't touch." Over the years, out of necessity, he's become an expert on deer-resistant plants. Rather than struggle to grow plants that the deer love, he's learned to grow what they don't eat. If you find out that the bully who steals your lunch every day doesn't like cream cheese and olive sandwiches, then by God, cream cheese and olive is what you pack every day.

"The only plants I lose are ones that I expect to be deer-resistant. They ate rue!" he says, shaking his head. "It's the most horrible-smelling plant there is." He has found that nonnative plants are often left alone by the deer. "By and large they don't like drought-resistant exotics, but every year there's a new plant they'll eat. They've now started to nibble on plants that were totally untouched in the seventies. And it's hard to plant natives because the deer evolved with them, and they've developed all this stuff to digest tannins and alkaloids."

Still, he's found plenty of plants that he can grow. Typical of his style is the long serpentine berm behind the house, which is filled with herbs and ornamentals, both native and exotic. It's all a beautiful experiment to find out how the plants will survive with minimal labor, fertilizer, and water.

"Because we get an average of fifty-eight inches of rain per year, some years as much as one hundred twenty inches, the problem is not the summer drought but winter drainage," Robert says. That's why he decided to try plant-

Foxglove and kniphofia provide color, and verbascum supplies the texture in a dense planting on Robert's berm.

ing on a mound. "First I dug out a serpentine area twelve to eighteen inches deep," he says. "Then I piled up wood chips and shredded tree refuse to a height of four feet. I covered it all with the topsoil I had removed and planted directly into it: pink, white, and blue rosemary, lavender, santolina, ornamental pampas grass. Then I used old newspaper to mulch everything and covered that with wood chips to hide the paper."

He did all the digging and planting in early fall and fin-

Taking garden writing a bit too literally, Robert has found that an old computer makes a perfect pot for thyme.

ished just before the rainy season. How does he know when the rainy season is about to start? "It's like that old joke," he explains. "Guy gets on the bus in an unfamiliar city and asks a stranger where to get off for the library. The stranger says, 'That's easy. Just watch me and get off one stop before I do.'"

Kourik explains what he had in mind for this huge bed. "My plan was to do no pruning or weeding for ten years," he says. "After seven or eight years, the wood chips had sunk two feet, and a few blackberry vines had found their way to the top, so I pulled them out. Granted, the lavender got woody on the bottom because I hadn't pruned, which all the magazines tell you to do. I just left the stems uncut."

But that laziness had an unexpected payoff. "One morning I went out, and on those bare stems there must have been a hundred, maybe a thousand, spider webs glowing and sparkling with dew in the morning sun. It was totally magical. And though it's happened only once in fifteen years, it was completely worth it."

Ten years after planting, he could call the experiment a success. "So I'm starting to prune things back. I replanted some lavender. Put in some *Stipa gigantea* so the western sun lights up the seed heads. I've planted three unusual types of cypress and a taller arbutus. I've tried three varieties of artemesia, but the deer ate them all. I keep trying to do more and more inspired laziness. I was a wild-man compulsive gardener when I moved here fifteen years ago. Not anymore. The ultimate goal is that nobody will recognize my landscape as a garden."

Much of Kourik's gardening strategy is to take advantage of existing plants, especially the massive tan bark oak that dominates the back yard. "It has three huge sweeping horizontal arms, like a great moss-covered sculpture," Robert says. "When I first moved here you couldn't even see those branches because of all the brush and the huckleberries. But I've cut back the brush, and I've pruned the

top curve of the huckleberries to mirror the curve of the tree."

That tree is also the centerpiece of a horticultural experiment. Kourik noticed that copious amounts of fog condensed on the leaves, then dripped to the ground. He wondered if the condensation could be used for irrigation. Over time he measured the amount of water, found that it was substantial, and now is planting to take advantage of it during the dry season. He calls it his fog-drip garden.

That kind of attention to the scientific method may be something Kourik learned from his father, John, an engineer. John is the kind of guy who not only counts but also measures and weighs the gumballs that fall from the two sweet gum trees in his yard in St. Louis. When Robert was growing up, his dad "was mainly a lawn guy. And I remember a vegetable garden with monstrous tomato hornworms that would scare me as a little kid. My dad says that he had to plant all the vegetables, and I just harvested (and ate)." Even then Robert was showing intimations of that inspired laziness. But he took over the lawn chores and went on to make a business out of it. "I mowed lawns like crazy, from two to five hours per week. First with a push mower until I could afford a riding mower. All through junior high school and high school."

He's still battling grass, mowing the grassland surrounding his garden to lessen the fire hazard. And he's thinking about installing a different type of lawn. "I've been working from natural models, and I'd like to put in a so-called lawn, five- to ten-feet wide, of *Artemesia californica*, commonly called sagebrush here. It is a true allelopathic plant, which in a pure stand doesn't allow the seeds of other plants to germinate. If I planted a strip of sagebrush, I would have an allelopathic border that would stop the march of grasslands toward my garden." Now that's inspired laziness.

In the fog-drip area, Robert gardens by subtraction, by

Across a small "lawn" of
mowed weeds and a dirt driveway, Robert's no-till berms are
thickly planted with several
types of lavender, foxglove,
and kniphofia.

pruning and shaping. "I took out all the western sword ferns, and I've pruned the native huckleberries. Except for three topiary huckleberries, nobody can recognize that I garden there. That, I think, is the ultimate compliment. Oh, some of the snooty visitors say, 'You don't have a designed garden.'" But others get it and appreciate the negative space. Some even note that he uses air as a design element.

This is a garden defined by its limitations, which Kourik recognizes and uses. He works with what he's been given: dry summers, clay soil, and deer. "Every three to four years I bring in a load of twenty yards of turkey manure. I spread it on top of my newspaper mulch. That and rice hulls and wood chips are my only input. Any watering is from the well. After ten years of sheet composting, I don't have to turn over any soil.

"I'm still trying to get people to try no-till, but that's difficult because people want to dig. They want to get their hands in the earth. Most people have a hard time planning and maintaining a natural garden. The difficulty comes with the need to keep their hands off, because our view of what's right doesn't always coincide with nature's way of doing things."

Here's Kourik on planning a natural garden. "Take a bunch of golf balls, throw them into the air, and where they land, that's where you plant a tree. Some will land close together, maybe two to three feet apart." That's natural spacing. "But for most of us," Kourik says, "it's hard to resist the urge to cheat and move some of the balls a little farther apart."

Kourik believes that most people don't have time to wait for a natural garden to develop, with no-till techniques and sheet composting, because we're such a mobile society. We have to work hard to get a garden to reach its peak quickly before we move on. "I sit on my mountaintop and watch suburbanites work on their gardens twenty or thirty times harder than I do."

He sits and watches a bobcat stalk a rabbit. Gets up in the morning early enough to hear the raccoons splashing in the water garden. And shrugs off the deer. "My garden is a wildlife corridor." He may work a bit on cutting some brush or carving out a hideout to replicate the fort he had under his grandmother's huge forsythia in Missouri.

In a way, his landscape does dredge up memories of childhood, when the natural world was filled with wonder. Back then nature was so perfect, we never thought of changing it. We wouldn't dream of trying to move a tree or improve upon the scene in any fashion. In a way, that's how Kourik deals with his surroundings. His hand is unseen here. He has checked his ego at the garden gate and doesn't feel the need to make a mark or carve his name into the trees.

A MAN'S GARDEN

JEFFREY BALE

PORTLAND, OREGON

In his neighborhood, Bale is known as the rock man. He often carries a bucket around to collect intriguing stones for his mosaics.

THIS AIN'T YOUR AVERAGE GUY'S garden party. No one has spent all afternoon mowing the lawn to within an inch of its life. Wait a minute, there isn't even any lawn in sight—the ground is covered with native and exotic plants, and stonework that's definitely exotic. There's no barbecue grill, no smell of sizzling meat. The flames are provided by scores of candles, and the scent is of jasmine. The sound doesn't come from a stereo or TV piped outside but from temple bells ringing in the wind. The pool is tiny; the only creatures swimming in it are koi.

(Opposite) Jeffrey Bale's version of a garden bed is literally a place to lie down and take a nap, reflecting his belief that the garden should be a place of peace and rest.

But, then, this ain't your average guy's garden, either. This small city lot in a rundown Portland neighborhood in the grip of gradual gentrification is unlike anything else around. Just walking by you're struck by the lushness of it. Year-round the landscape looks like a jungle trying to break free of its bounds. The front yard is packed with greenery—mahonia, vine maples, rhododendrons, and hydrangeas. Potted plants line the handsome river-stone

77

dala, Bale reclines like the hookah-smoking caterpillar in *Alice in Wonderland.*

He has just returned from India and the Far East, and he seems sufficiently chilled out. For twelve years he has been traveling to that mystical part of the world, soaking up the cultures, studying the religions, visiting temples and gardens, learning from artisans. Exploring. "I found a village in southern India where they've been carving granite for two thousand years. There are over a hundred shops in this little village. You walk around, and all you hear is the chinking sound of hammer and chisel."

Bale worked with some artisans there to design some garden statuary. "I wanted to do an adaptation of Hindu concepts that would work well in the garden. So I designed a bowl that's perfectly round, with a carved lotus blossom inside to symbolize enlightenment."

Enlightenment is what he searches for on his travels. In

(Above) Though trained in a conventional landscape architecture program, Bale found that he had to strike out on his own path to create the types of gardens that resonated within him.

(Right) Bale believes that the four elements — air, earth, fire, and water — should be represented in the garden. The mosaic path represents earth, and the small pond water. The pond also attracts wildlife to the garden.

steps: bamboo, ginger, *Hakonechloa.* When you step into the yard from the sidewalk, you feel as if you're entering a refuge.

That's the way Jeffrey Bale planned it. At the party, you'll likely find him reclining on a bed, a real honest-to-goodness sleeping bed covered with silk pillows and framed by a bamboo arch hung with temple bells. Wearing an Indian skull cap and a T-shirt emblazoned with a man-

India, when they travel they don't go on vacations, they go on pilgrimages. For me travel, is being able to visit places that inspire me, make me dream."

Yes, he brings back carvings and statues and relics, but he also brings back a certain mindset. "When I get back from India I have a festival." Thus this garden party.

"I make an Indian buffet and put carpets and pillows all over the garden to create a paradise. It's a Mogul idea. The idea is that friends come here and everyone exists in paradise for a day, to connect with the magic that can be created in a garden." This is Jeffrey Bale's conception of heaven on earth. The bed is a big part of it. It's important, he says, to take a horizontal approach to the garden.

"In Persian gardens you lie down on carpets in a very comfortable setting so you can meditate. In the English-style garden we sit on a hard bench and we're always thinking about what needs to be done next," he says. "You talk to people about gardens, and maintenance is their first consideration. They just want it to look nice and tidy and impress the neighbors and make their house look more valuable." That's not his approach.

This is a garden in the purest sense, based on a very ancient concept. "There are beautiful gardens in India that are models of heaven," he says. "Mogul kings built tombs that are models of paradise, incorporating huge gardens so that when they died they would move into paradise and become gods. And I think you can design a home garden along those lines."

That's what he's done in this small Portland lot. Bale believes that to make the perfect garden, it's essential to incorporate the four elements of nature: air, fire, water, earth. The air is always there, of course, and invisible. But Bale makes people aware of it by hanging temple bells throughout his garden. "In Thailand they put bells on temples, and when the wind spirits pass through they ring the bells. Whenever the wind blows it draws your conscious-

The garden is an extremely spiritual place for Bale. He believes that good gardens incorporate art, so every year he brings back statuary from his pilgrimages to the Far East.

ness to that experience. It's something very magical whenever the bells ring."

For water, his garden has a small, rock-lined pond full of fish. As they swim and jump and splash, they make you aware of the water. For fire, there are lanterns and candles, their flames flickering in the night. "I have even built fire pits," Jeffrey says, "but in an urban context, neighbors often call the fire department when they smell smoke."

A MAN'S GARDEN

Earth is easy, of course. It's under everything. But he has brought the earthy element to the forefront with his use of stone, especially in his pebble mosaics, which are the heart of this garden. Mosaics dominate the back yard, creating a swirling piece of art underfoot, with hundreds of stones, tiles, and river rocks winding around one another in earth colors of gray, silver, and blue.

For Jeffrey the mosaics have deep mystical undertones. "I started to do an abstract representation of time and space and physics," he says, "so that when you look at them they represent a connection with the cosmos. The stones are different colors relating to different times of the year. Black is the color of winter, for example. For me, doing mosaics in native stone creates a local connection. Around here everybody knows me as the rock man. I'm known for always having a bucket with me."

His mosaics offer a connection not only to nature and the cosmos but to his personal heritage as well. "My grandparents on both sides were rockhounds," he says. "On their vacations they would gather rocks. Their yards were filled with them. In fact, one of my grandfathers built a big fireplace out of lava rocks and shells and created a kind of work of art."

Jeffrey shares his vision by creating mosaics and gardens for others. "I had a dream of doing a Persian-carpet mosaic," he says. "And I finally did one for a client. It's my masterpiece. It's a paradise carpet where you can sit and meditate. It blends Hindu, Buddhist, and Islamic concepts into an American patio. Just the process of sorting stones

(Opposite) Bale combines native plants like mahonia, an underused plant in his opinion, with exotics such as pampas grass and ordinary annuals like impatiens.

becomes a meditation." He likes to involve his clients in the creation of the mosaics. "I did one garden for people who wanted a path for a new entry to their house," he says. "So I created a mosaic mandala that they will have to pass over every day. It will trigger a consciousness out into the world and get them thinking differently than they would normally. It will be like passing through a heavenly paradise on the way to work."

That was a bit more than the clients had bargained for. They would have settled for something pretty. "But their kids were really into it," he says. "I told them you have to go out and gather stones in very special places and have great experiences in nature so you'll have memories attached to those things. It was wonderful. We gathered all these wonderful stones, and I made the kids sort them by color. I talked about where I was going to place them, and I did a ritual of lighting incense and casting the mosaic wheel. And the kids really got into it."

His designs, whether in stone or in plant material, are about much more than pleasing a client or even pleasing the human eye. His designs contain something that is missing from most garden design in America: a mystical reason for being. They obey a higher natural law. Pay attention, because this gets a little wild.

"There's an incredible diversity in this world," Jeffrey says earnestly. "But it's all made of the same thing. Buddha feels the connection of all things. So you have to build a space that relates cosmically to everything. Like the temple at Angkor Watt which is built on an enormous cosmic pattern. It relates to the sun and moon and constellations. The gods will move into this grid and inhabit it."

That's the goal of the garden. Sure beats the heck out of having a nice place for a barbecue.

In Jeffrey's small garden on a 1,400-square-foot lot, you can see what he calls "the magic of nature." The four elements are united. The native plants attract birds. Wasps sip water from the pond and the fish eat harmful bugs. The

The tiny back yard is entirely isolated from the rest of this urban neighborhood by judicious lush plantings of natives and exotics. Bale believes that a garden should be a retreat where one can escape from the world.

air carries the scent of daphnes, kiwi blossoms, and honeysuckle and the sound of temple bells.

"You realize that it's all connected, and you're connected to it." Somehow this brings us back to the bed. "You really have to lie down to appreciate that," he says.

This is the garden before it was shaped by European influences, put through the grinder of American sensibility and necessity. And yes, this garden stands out here, but people like it. "People driving by stop their cars to get a better look," Jeffrey says. "Asian people will stop and stare at the house because they hear the temple bells. And people walking by stop to touch the stones. It's just a little garden in the ghetto, but hundreds of people want to see it. "I've been approached to be on the three major citywide garden tours."

Jeffrey operates a thriving landscape design business. Some people might say that five clients a year does not make him a success, but he doesn't want to work with more clients than that. In fact, when people seek him out, he interviews them rather than the other way around.

"I built a garden for a client last year based entirely on Persian concepts of paradise," he says. "I put in a bathtub and plumbed it with hot water. There's a lotus pool with lotus blossoms. There are fountains creating sound. It's filled with fragrant plants. The people sleep out there. They take all their baths out there. They eat out there. And the garden has completely changed their lives."

Eastern mysticism meets Western practicality in Jeffrey Bale's gardens. Indian carvings and Buddha statues meet native Oregon plants. "I have a strong base in native plants," he says. "Ron Livinger was my mentor at the University of Oregon. He traveled all over the world. He really knows how to express the vernacular and sense of place, so that when you enter a garden you know where you are. And even though I'm using exotic elements, my gardens are based on my environment."

A favorite native is the cascara tree. He has one growing in front of his house, and it's special. "My mother lives on an old farm, and I dug some cascaras from her property and brought them here. Collecting plants from nature, you get a different genetic pool," he says. And because it's a

(Opposite) Mosaics are a hallmark of Bale's gardens. He encourages his clients to gather stones for their gardens from significant places.

THE MEDITATIVE MAN

A large cascara tree hides Bale's house from the street. He favors this native for its fragrance and its attraction for birds.

native plant, "native birds are really attracted to it." he says.

"I've got a good representation of Willamette Valley natives here. I've got maples. I've got mahonia. I love mahonias. I think they're underused. Even though they're the state flower of Oregon, people here don't appreciate them enough."

That's not to say his yard is an exclusively native enclave. He has plenty of exotics as well, including plants for the hot summer. "*Clerodendrum*, harlequin glory-bower, is great because it blooms in August when it's really hot here."

He even has plants for winter. In December and January the perfume from *Sarcococea*, sweet box, is overpowering. Other favorite scented plants are daphnes, akebia vine, and *Actinidia deliciosa*, Arctic-beauty kiwi, which has a really beautiful smell. He also has a big wisteria growing in an old rotting cherry tree.

"Akebia is a favorite because it's very clean, and I like to keep maintenance down. That's why I rarely use roses except rugosas. They have nice fall color, and I like that because I want to get the most out of plants that I can. I use euphorbias a lot. They are fascinating plants. I use hellebores. I like winter bloomers because I think you need that hopefulness that flowers represent in winter. I don't use tulips. But I use things that will naturalize and bloom early in spring. *Leucojum*—snowflakes—have a wonderful form and are so flashy. I like small narcissus, sometimes crocus, winter aconites."

Jeffrey has been dabbling in the tropical look, too. "Instead of buying petunias or other annuals, I'll buy houseplants like parlor palms, and stick them in the garden. They won't winter over, but I'm just using them as annuals."

Like many men who garden, Bale had it in his blood. It just bubbled out a little differently than it does for most men. "My grandfather was really into gardening. He lived in Bend, Oregon, a dry, hot, difficult place to garden. But he loved petunias." He pauses for a minute and you can sense him recalling an olfactory memory. "They smelled wonderful," he says a bit dreamily. And that leads him to the memory of another flower. "Sweet peas," he says, smiling. "My grandfather's garden was sensually a wonderful place. In an arid climate, he had an oasis." Somewhat like Bale's garden in a blighted urban landscape. There was a food garden, too. "A half-acre, not aesthetically pleasing, and I was an indentured servant there."

By the time Jeffrey was in junior high school, gardening —landscaping nature—had become an obsession. "For a school project, I interviewed a landscape architect. I just knew that's what I wanted to be." He studied the subject at the University of Oregon. "I got perfect scores all the time in my plant classes. It was just natural. I was lucky that way." When he graduated he took a job in a landscape design firm. "And I lasted about fifteen minutes," he says. "I sat at my desk, and they wanted me to draw little cars in a parking lot for a veterans' hospital." That was not what he had gone to school for; it had nothing to do with what he loved: plants and nature. "I felt as if I had been sentenced to prison." He could see his whole life flashing before his eyes, so he dropped his pen and left. "It was a sunny day and I went running down the street."

He's never looked back. "I started my own business. Basically I was pulling weeds for five dollars an hour and starving while learning how to do a little tile cutting and mosaic work."

Now people seek him out for his imaginative take on gardening. He doesn't advertise; he has no Web site. "It's all by word of mouth," he says. "People really respond to my gardens." There's a bit of wonderment in his voice. He knows that he's pretty far out, quite a bit to the left of the mainstream. "But I'm relating to the universe—that's the ultimate form of design. Most people who study gardening learn how to grow a certain kind of plant, or maybe how to combine colors. But I think you need to start from another direction, a deeper knowledge, from the basic primordial beginnings and connection to nature."

That may be beyond the grasp of many people. In truth, most men don't quite get it. "I generally deal with wives," Jeffrey says. "The men say, 'What about the sprinkler system?' and 'What do you mean you're taking my lawn away?'" But everyone can respond to the beauty of Bale's gardens. "Whenever I do a garden, I guarantee it will be beautiful, and it will change your life because the beauty will inspire you. That is essential. It has to be beautiful. That's my one unconditional guarantee."

When John and Christina Craighead moved into their Vermont
home, John immediately installed
an entry garden, using shrubs,
heathers, and grasses that would
remain attractive year-round.

The swimming pool once stuck out like a sore thumb in the Craigheads' front yard, but now it's surrounded by a lush border of annuals and perennials, including Russian sage, achillea, cimicifuga, phlox, and snapdragons.

JOHN CRAIGHEAD

FERRISBURGH, VERMONT

JOHN CRAIGHEAD IS SITTING on top of the world. Seated near the crest of a 1,000-foot-high hilltop in Vermont, he can believe he is master of all he sees. Lake Champlain glistens below, and beyond, to the west, the peaks of the Adirondacks pierce the sky. John is enjoying the view from, appropriately enough, an Adirondack chair on his rolling lawn.

When he stands up, John is taller and thinner than you expect. With his gray hair and beard, he resembles a dignified John Voight. He looks like a man who would play handball on Sunday mornings and win. He seems refined, yet his hair is gathered into a short ponytail. He is, in short, a man of contradictions.

In the mid-1990s John and his wife, Christina, bought this large property with one of the most beautiful views in the Champlain Valley. You might think he would be satisfied to sit and enjoy the scenery with a drink in his hand.

The expansive front lawn allows visitors to sit among the birches in the
evening and enjoy the view of Lake Champlain and the Adirondacks,
while the scent from the nicotiana border settles over them.

But no. John Craighead sees this beautiful setting as a problem to be solved. For he is a scientist, a problem solver. For him, this landscape is a challenge on several fronts.

First, there is the climate. Yes, it can be beautiful here . . . for all of two weeks in midsummer. Sure, the winters are invigorating. The thigh-deep snow is fantastic for skiing around the property. And the spring mud . . . well, that's not good for anything. Barely on the fringes of Zone 4, even in a good year this place is hard on gardens. The winter wind whips off the lake, desiccating the plants, and temperatures can drop into the minus twenties. In spring the temperature may plummet thirty degrees overnight.

Plenty of people garden in Vermont, of course. But most play it safe. They wait for the all-clear on Memorial Day and stuff their gardens with marigolds, petunias, impatiens, and other annuals. Some of the more adventurous grow the tried-and-true perennials and shrubs: peonies, iris, lupines, and lilac. Not John. He welcomes the difficulty of the climate as a learning experience and a way to make a contribution. And if his efforts bring him some attention, well, that's fine, too.

For this professor emeritus of pathology at the University of Vermont, all the world is a laboratory. And the landscape spread out before him is a multidimensional theorem to be solved. The plants are the variables.

He is not content to merely create an attractive garden, he needs to have a mission. "I think we have a lot to learn about northern climates," he says, "and I plan to use this garden as a model. I'm a scientist by training. I view plants as a challenge—a scientific challenge, an artistic challenge, and a planning challenge." Listening to him, you feel as though you are in a laboratory, or at least a classroom, rather than wandering through a gorgeous home garden.

His goal of learning about plants helps to explain why he has such a variety of them. He is testing them against

John couldn't experiment with all the exotic cultivars he desired unless he could grow them from seed, so he designed and built an elaborate six-tier seed-starting table.

the climate and against one another. "There is such a diversity of plant material," he says, "and that is an opportunity for experimentation." He shrugs. "It's all trial and error."

Others might be content to just plant and enjoy. Not John. "You must consider and take advantage of all aspects of plants," he explains. "Flowers and structure, leaves and bark. You have to piece all those things to-

89

THE SCIENTIST

Masses of annuals, such as zinnias and ageratum, are an important part of this man's garden. He wants to make an impact with a long, bright blooming season in his short-summer climate.

gether in a continuum of the seasons. And still you're not finished."

Okay, so he makes gardening sound about as romantic and appealing as taking an algebra exam. But in fact, the total effect is much prettier than his stated intention makes it sound.

As you drive up the steep, winding gravel driveway toward the house, a view of the lake appears in your rearview mirror. But your eyes are drawn ahead to a thick row of pink cleome, standing like sentinels before a metal sculpture. As the driveway bends to the right, the flower beds explode into view in a conflagration of midsummer colors. There are lots of pastels, pinks, and purples, combined with whites. Annuals like snapdragons and asters are mixed in with perennials like monarda and cimicifuga.

When you get out of the car, you're in an entry garden that feels welcoming at any time of year. This garden was John's first project after moving into the house. First he ripped up the old driveway and moved it to a place that wasn't so obtrusive, and then he installed an entry garden that would provide interest year-round, even in this hard climate. And that's not easy.

Problem: the cold, windy climate curtails the number of plants that will survive. Solution: if you are experimenting with specimens of questionable hardiness, plant them in the sheltered entry garden.

"It's a major undertaking to have something blooming here from May to October," John says. But he wasn't satisfied with just a six-month garden. "It's a long bleak winter, so I wanted to emphasize winter interest. I'm trying out various shrubs, so that when all the flowers are gone, you have something to look at. *Ilex* is a good choice for that. As are ornamental grasses, pines, heather." Even hydrangeas, with their flowerheads left on to dry, are attractive all winter.

This garden has conifers for structure and redbuds for spring color. In spring there are violas and fritillarias, while summer features gaudy caladiums and primroses. But shrubs and trees are the real backbone of the entry garden: ginkgo, stewartia, smokebush, and plenty of viburnums. There's rose of Sharon (dicey here) brought from Nantucket, while ground-hugging heathers provide interest through the rough winter months.

John likes his plantings lush and long-lasting, so he combines annuals
and perennials in the borders. He also picks many of the annuals for
flower arrangements.

91

92

Problem: the cold, windy climate curtails human activity. No matter how attractive the plants are in winter, here in Vermont you want to enjoy them from inside a warm house. Solution: build a conservatory.

Thinking of winter, John added a huge glass room jutting off the south side of the house. The conservatory is a perfect place to soak up the reduced light of winter and surround yourself with greenery when all outside is brown and white. It's a great place to browse through seed catalogs.

Then, of course, John had to landscape around the conservatory.

Problem: a hard-to-maintain, difficult-to-traverse slope beside the house. Solution: bring in rocks and earth and large machines.

"My vision was to have a soft slope with lots of plants," says John. "So we brought in truckloads of rocks." Not just stones but huge chunks of Vermont ledge. Tons of them, to build a terrace with stone steps. What better way, as a man, to make your mark, than to move a huge amount of earth and transform the landscape?

That was just the start. The once-solid lawn surrounding the house is now studded with flower beds. Each has a different emphasis, from the vegetable beds behind the house to the shade garden and rock garden on the north, the pool garden on the east, and Christina's mixed island beds on the south.

Problem: aesthetic differences between husband and wife. "My wife has the artistic interest, and I'm more interested in plant materials," John says. "It is an effective partnership. Though we do have our arguments. She doesn't like yellow and orange, for example, but I do."

(Opposite) Fall is foliage season in Vermont, but it's also a time when the garden peters out. John has worked hard to incorporate plants such as sedum that remain attractive well into the fall.

Solution: give her two beds on the south side of the house for whites and pastels. Take charge of all the rest, including the meadow on the north side, which is a huge canvas of yellows, oranges, and blues. Planted with John's own custom mix, the meadow was inspired by fields the Craigheads walked through in Tuscany.

In fact, walking the garden with John is like taking a quick botanic tour of the world. The beds are studded with plants brought back from the Craigheads' travels in South Africa, the Andes, New Zealand, Asia, and Europe. Stroll the garden with him, and it's clear that it's more than a laboratory. This place is a trophy garden. He loves to boast about the plants and seeds he's brought back from exotic locales.

"We were over in Tuscany years ago, and they had fields and fields of Shirley poppies with cornflowers and you couldn't imagine how beautiful those were. I'd love to simulate that," he says. He has a plant they first saw growing wild in the Alps. And "when we were in China there were fields of these Chinese forget-me-nots that you could wander through."

Now a few of those plants are growing here in northern Vermont. Wherever John goes he's on the lookout for plants that will thrive in this climate. He thinks alpines could be the answer, with more study.

"We need a laboratory for alpines," he says. And he intends for his garden to be it.

Problem: a dearth of alpine plants available from nurseries. Solution: grow them from seed. "An enormous number of alpine seeds are available," John says. He's built a sophisticated, practically fail-safe seed-starting setup in the new barn to take advantage of them. It has three levels, with six adjustable fluorescent bulbs on each level. "It works out beautifully," he says. "You can raise the height. You don't depend on the sun. I'd recommend it to anyone."

The seed-starting trays are also where he raises most of the transplants for his huge vegetable garden beside the

93

barn, where everything grows in neat, wooden-sided raised beds.

Problem: shallow, flinty soil. Or, as John puts it in his professorial way: "This monadnock soil profile is not propitious to spading." Solution: raised beds filled with a combination of compost, turkey manure, and trucked-in topsoil. "I decided that raised beds are the approach to take. Raised beds are an extraordinary way to deal with problems."

Like the rest of the landscape here, the vegetable garden is full of interesting and exotic yet unlike plants, all thrown together in an experimental mix. It looks great, but John is hypercritical. "I liked the idea of experimenting with bringing flowers and vegetables together," he says. "But since everything doesn't blossom and mature at the same time, well, not every plan works out the way you'd like it to."

The vegetable garden has a dozen beds, and you might find nasturtiums in bed with broccoli, Russian kale, and fava beans, or castor beans rubbing elbows with carrots. Beans grow alongside nicotiana, and asparagus shares a bed with asters. You'll find cleome growing with strawberries. There's a huge datura in the potato bed. Right in the middle is a nursery bed covered with lathe where perennial seedlings are sent to harden off.

So every bed is an experiment. Lots of plants are thrown together to see what works. It's like the way a lot of guys approach cooking. And if some plant doesn't work? Get rid of it. Tea roses too fussy and transient? Boom, out they go, to be replaced by English roses. The shade bed gives way to a rock garden. The lime-green Queen Anne's lace gives way to nicotiana of the same color. The variegated elderberry is moved around until it finds a place it likes, tucked in beside the barn.

Problem: how do you experiment with plants in a harsh climate and still keep the garden looking good? For John, the garden is not so much about design but about the plants themselves. Design is the equation, but plants are the numbers that fill it in and make it work. Solution: annuals. John mixes annuals and perennials with impunity. He mixes colors and heights and textures as well. With enough variety, the odds are a bed will look good most of the time. There are a certain number of plants available and a certain number of conditions that must be met. Put the two together and you have a solution. And a great-looking garden.

Take the pool garden, for instance. It's a lush mishmash of species and varieties of perennials and annuals. There are mounds of 'Peaches and Cream' snapdragons cheek by jowl with huge, billowing hedges of Russian sage. Cardinal vine climbs the pool house, cimicifuga battles cleome for attention. There are daylilies, globe thistles, phlox, monarda, and more.

The garden is so bright and exuberant that it actually draws your eye away from the mountain view beyond. And that brings us to the final problem. It's a huge, unspeakable problem for a gardener, like the elephant in the living room. That problem is The View.

The view, of course, is fantastic. It's breathtaking at sunset, especially in autumn. It's glorious in winter when the first snow falls on the Adirondack peaks. The problem, though, is that it is borrowed. Really, anybody with enough money and good vision can have a view. But you can't own it, you can't take credit for it. And you can't take pride in your own garden if the view overwhelms it.

What good is it to entertain, to throw garden parties, if people can't tear their eyes away from the sunset over the lake? You just want to discuss plants. You want to boast a little bit about what you've done. But how can your efforts compete with nature?

You host a meeting of the Hardy Plant Society or are included on the local garden tour, and the visitors politely volunteer their appreciation of your garden, but their eyes are always drawn toward the horizon. So what can you

do? Make your landscape interesting. Fill it full of bright, exotic plants. And strive to keep it looking good year-round. Because that view is always there, competing for attention.

John Craighead had to put his own stamp on this property, had to mark it as his. And he has succeeded. When you turn your lawn chair around, away from the hills, you realize that the view in the opposite direction, with the house sitting on a rolling lawn surrounded by beds bursting with color, is every bit as enticing as the view to the west.

Wallenborn counts on cannas to brighten up his lush garden. Sun-loving coleus are among his pet plants, too.

A MAN'S GARDEN

PETER WALLENBORN

ASHEVILLE, NORTH CAROLINA

Peter Wallenborn loves color. His three-level garden in North Carolina is peppered with dahlias, which he enters in flower shows.

WHEN PETER WALLENBORN STARTED working in his yard a dozen years ago in a suburb of Asheville, he belonged to the "All I know about gardening I learned on the golf course" school of landscape design. He had never gardened before. His parents had never gardened. None of his friends gardened. To many of the guys in the neighborhood, any kind of gardening outside of lawn care seemed like a sissy thing, woman's work.

Wallenborn's early brushes with "nature" were from the far end of a nine-iron. As a teenager, the only times he thought about landscaping were when he was on the golf course. That, he thought, must have been the way the Garden of Eden looked, or heaven itself. The golf course was his natural ideal.

As a member of the high school golf team, Peter had the chance to play some of the prettiest courses in the state. He was dazzled by the bright neon-green grass, the tall white pines, the azaleas blooming in the spring. Peter may have been the only one on the team who appreciated the look of the course. And as he waited for a partner to line up a putt or address the ball, he'd admire the landscaping. At the same time, he couldn't help but think about how he would improve it if given the chance. "When I played courses, I was always looking at the holes and trying to figure out what would make them prettier," he says.

Something about those long stretches of turf, undulating hills, and stately trees touched the young Peter Wal-

(Left) The name "Peter" means rock, and this Peter has constructed hundreds of feet of rock walls snaking through his gardens.

(Opposite) Wherever there's a sunny spot, Peter has planted dahlias, here alongside a clump of pampas grass.

lenborn, as it was meant to. The courses are designed to provide golfers a feeling of peace. They are designed to awaken some distant memory of simple joy from our childhood. Some say they even evoke a racial memory of the childhood of our species on the savannas of Africa.

As men, however, we immediately start thinking about how we would change the landscape and put our own stamp on it. For a time Peter seriously entertained the notion of becoming a golf course designer. But the college he had chosen didn't offer courses in landscape architecture. Since he couldn't play God by designing golf courses, he did the next best thing. He became a surgeon.

In his early years of medical school and residency, there was barely time for golf, never mind gardening. The landscape was something that flashed by on his way to the hospital. But eventually his life settled down, and he and

his wife started a family and bought a house in the suburbs—with a yard, of course.

That's when Wallenborn faced the decision that would change his life: golf clubs or hand tools? Should he hire a landscaper and let somebody else mow and clip the hedges while he perfected his game? Or should he do a little gardening? Maybe a lot of gardening. Maybe remake the yard to give it the mark of his own individuality.

He chose to make a mark on the land. He didn't do it all at once, because he couldn't afford to. "We had bought a house with no landscaping at all," Peter explains. "We didn't have much income, either. So I bought some inexpensive plants and started playing around in the yard." And though this planting satisfied an urge, something else was pulling at him. Something more permanent. It had to do with rocks. "While I was planting, I also started building walls with quarry rock." And he found that he couldn't stop building them. Before Peter knew it, he had run out of space in the garden and, with two kids and a third on the way, in the house. So he and the family moved to a bigger house with a bigger yard in the same neighborhood.

The new yard offered Peter a chance to start over again, to create something from nothing. The front yard was already landscaped in the typical southern suburban style: big lawn, foundation plants, specimen trees, and a few shrubs.

The back, though, was a disaster—inaccessible and almost unusable. A sharp drop-off, dangerous to navigate

A MAN'S GARDEN

(Opposite) There are few open spaces and almost no lawn in this junglelike garden, so Peter has to squeeze in sitting areas where he can. A potted banana plant conveys a tropical feel.

(Right) A little bit of lawn provides the negative space to set off the colors of cannas, rudbeckia, and echinacea.

and overgrown with brush and scrub, led to a swampy area filled with weeds and a few scrubby locust trees. The kind of place you tell your kids to stay away from. But one man's neglected back yard is another man's opportunity for creation. Once Peter saw that yard (and the old English-style greenhouse attached to the house) he knew he had to have it.

Today, the landscape that faces the street hasn't changed much. It still has that par-three fairway look. The lawn is bright green and always trim. There are formal boxwoods and a weeping cherry or two. This is the face Peter turns toward the neighbors. It is perfectly acceptable, quite ordinary, and allows him to conform to the aesthetic norms of the neighborhood. That's important for the man running with the suburban pack of other guys. We

must strive to belong. We can't appear to be too different or we will be ostracized and perhaps even considered dangerous. Thus the cookie-cutter foundation plantings in suburbs from coast to coast.

But in the back yard, well, that's a different story. The back yard is Peter's own private creation. It's a crazy quilt of eye-opening color on three different levels. It's an eclectic collection of hundreds of species of plants, most of them flowering. And most of them flower at the same time, it seems, in contrasting colors. It's a kaleidoscope bursting with the bright primary colors a man loves. It's also an active, muscle-flexing garden. An earth-moving, rock-wall-building garden.

This garden is like the loud flannel shirt with the holes in the elbows that a guy wears around the house on the weekend. This is where the surgeon gets his hands dirty, lets his hair down, and plays. This, Peter says, sweeping his arm to encompass the garden, "is an enjoyable and relaxing stress reliever. When I'm out in the garden, I'm away from the phone. There's no time line. There are no deadlines." In one very important way it couldn't be more removed from his work. "Out here, if something dies it's not a problem," he says. It might take a while to even notice that it has died. The lot, less than an acre in size, is jammed with more than eight hundred species of plants, each screaming for attention.

If there's a plan at work here it's not immediately evident. "They say you should repeat different plants in groups throughout the garden," Peter notes, "but I just don't have enough garden space to repeat groups of plants. In most cases I probably don't have more than two plants of each species. So what I do is repeat combinations of colors in different plants." The result is dazzling. Or dizzying. Prize-winning dahlias shout, "Look at me!" but the asters next to them demand your attention as well.

Still, it all works, in a very masculine kind of way. Though most of his neighbors wouldn't understand why he spends his time here rather than on the golf course or in front of the TV, lots of old-time guy gardeners would feel right at home here. The colors would comfort them. There is something about this garden that's a throwback to earlier days. It couldn't be farther from a natural garden.

It's remarkable how much Peter has accomplished in just a few years. The back yard was his challenge, his chance to make his own creation.

First he had to drain and fill the swamp. So he got out a spade and a pair of heavy boots and went to work digging drainage ditches and installing drain tile. Then he had the city dump truckload after truckload of leaves into the ravine, and he brought in several truckloads of topsoil. "I had them dump piles of dirt where I wanted island beds."

In time Peter created a firmament out of nothing. And he designed it as a little world with its own logic and rules and seasons and time. "My plan was to create a kind of harmony and to try to make a garden year-round." He also wanted to create the illusion of a larger world behind the house. He wanted to generate the feeling "that you could never see the entire garden from any one place," he says. "I wanted to entice people to keep moving and wonder what's around the next corner."

As he stands at street level and looks down on his creation, he says, "My gardening sense is a gift I was given. I've just exploited it and have used it to try to encourage others to enjoy gardening. "My garden is my artwork. The creativity is what I love about it. Walking around and seeing that it really looks beautiful, knowing that it's all something that I created is very satisfying."

For many men, that satisfaction is greatest, or at least the payoff most obvious, when the garden is bright and bold. Bright colors, and lots of them, make their accomplishments in the garden easy to see, easy to brag about. And you don't have to be a fussy, compulsive gardener to earn that kind of payoff.

"I'm not a perfectionist back there," Wallenborn says. "I don't even have a plan. It's more of a collection of favorite plants, of what strikes me from year to year, than it is a designed garden."

What strikes him is not subtle hues or foliage or form, but colorful flowers. Like dahlias, a favorite plant year after year. "They make great cut flowers," he says. "I generally have them all over the house and in the operating room and in the office. I like big bold colors. It's hard to beat dahlias when they're healthy, and when you have the right conditions for them."

Of all the hundreds of plants in the garden, the dahlias get the most pampering. Though their tubers would sur-

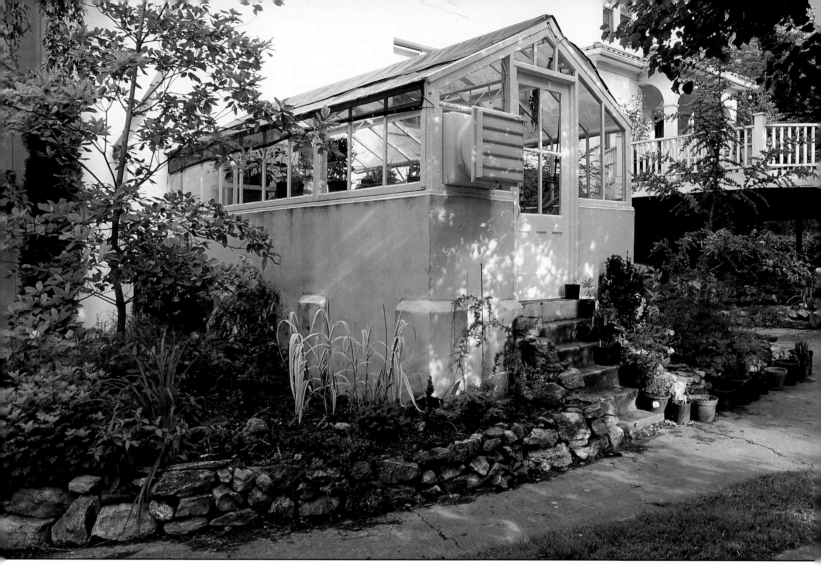

When he saw the attached greenhouse, Peter knew he had to buy this house. He uses the greenhouse to start seeds and take cuttings of his prize coleus.

vive the winter in the ground in Asheville, he still digs them each fall. "I have so many unusual types. It would be too much of a risk to leave them in the ground. I'm afraid they would rot, so I dig them up and divide them. It takes me about seven or eight hours just to dig them."

He amends the soil in the dahlia bed every year with alpaca manure and potash. With all that care the blooms earn him plenty of recognition. He's known in certain cir-

Peter has tamed his hilly property by clearing brush and breaking the steep slope into terraces held by rock walls and planted with colorful perennials.

cles as the dahlia guy. He exhibits the huge flowers in local shows. "But I'm not really in it for the competition or the notoriety," he says.

It's true that something about dahlias can set a man's heart to beating faster. Something about that big, bold flower speaks to us—the bright primary colors, the spiky petals. It's elemental. When you say "flower," dahlia blooms jump to mind. Forget your muted hues, your simple forms, your diminutive spikelets with their insignificant flowers. No, when we say "flower," we mean dahlia.

Along with dahlias, Peter grows cannas and zinnias, and now he enjoys the splashy colors of coleus, especially the unusual sun-loving varieties—his latest infatuation. "For about three years I've been growing sun-loving coleus." Because they are somewhat rare, they get a bit of special treatment as well. "It's hard to find some of the varieties," he says. "So I take cuttings from them and grow them in the greenhouse over the winter so I'll have them the following year."

"I'm somewhat of a collector," Peter says. "If I read about a plant in a magazine and it sounds good, I try to find it and grow it." But each plant has to work for him, and he doesn't show a lot mercy to those that aren't well adapted to his garden. "I'll try a new plant twice, and if it dies twice then I forget it."

He's got fifty varieties of dahlias. And when they're blooming the garden blazes. There are eight varieties of butterfly bushes. "I also have 150 to 200 types of conifers. Most have done fine here. I've got plants that generally like a colder climate, like lilacs. Canna lilies will survive the winter here without mulching . I have a lot of tropical plants that grow outside in summer: a giant banana plant and a tree fern that's about twelve feet tall."

He's keenly aware of, and grateful for, Asheville's benign climate. "You can grow just about anything around here. I've even got six different types of daphnes, which they say you can't grow here. But I've been very successful with them," he says proudly.

Though it's hard to imagine how he could cram in any more plants, he says the garden is not done. Probably never will be. "It's evolving," he says. "I'm always looking to see if something doesn't look quite right. Then I ask myself, 'What do I need, a rock wall, an evergreen . . .?' My tastes change every year. One year I may concentrate on sun-loving coleus, one year evergreens. So the garden looks different every year."

The plants receive most of Peter's attention, of course, but plants do die. They grow old, they become diseased, they fall out of favor, and they get pulled out. But rocks are forever. With rocks and rocks walls, you can really make a lasting monument. And Peter has lots of rocks.

"My specialty is rock work," he says. "Maybe that's because the name Peter means rock." At his first house, before he put a single plant in the ground, he started building walls. Those walls still stand, a dozen years after he moved out. And at this house, rock walls snake through the property on every level. "I guess there must be one hundred tons of rock down there. I have some property out in the Blue Ridge Mountains near the national park. That property just about grows rocks. So whenever I go out there I load up my truck and bring some back. When I get enough I build another wall.

"I'm really not a perfectionist in the garden," he repeats, perhaps protesting a bit too much. "People look at my garden and say, 'This is terribly obsessive/compulsive,' but really, I let all my plants grow together. It's true that in the summer I like to have everything looking good, and I have container plants that I move around. That's part of making all parts of the garden look good year-round. But I'm not compulsive. As a surgeon, I have to be, but not here."

ROGER CLARKSON

RIVERSIDE, CALIFORNIA

DOUG JOHNSON

EAST MONTPELIER, VERMONT

SOMETIMES A LAWNMOWER and a leaf blower are just not enough to satisfy a guy's need to play with toys in the garden. In that case drastic measures are called for. It's time to dig trenches, pour ballast, string wires, and lay track. A few days and a few thousand dollars later, the landscape has been transformed. It has a new life, a raison d'être. The garden now has a model train running through it.

Don't laugh. As quirky as it may seem, railroad gardening is one of the fastest-growing garden activities in America. Today it's not hard to find a back (or even a front) yard where the Super Chief roars past hillsides covered with lemon thyme or through a forest of miniature spruce or past pansies with blossoms as big as a house — a miniature house, that is. That's railroad gardening. It's a world populated by dwarf plants, G-scale trains, miniature villages, and tiny figurines.

Roger Clarkson's garden railroad is built on a platform of steel and cement, with hundreds of yards of dirt trucked in. He figures he's spent more than a hundred thousand dollars on his hobby.

Cedars, spruce, and a Norfolk
pine stand like sentinels over the
Clarkson train yard.

There are hundreds of garden railway clubs in America. The magazine *Garden Railways* has seen its circulation soar since its inception in 1984. From coast to coast there is a whole subculture of railroad gardeners.

It's not surprising to learn that this unique pastime was born from a combination of British quirkiness and German engineering. Transplant that combo across the ocean and feed it with a good dose of American obsessiveness, and you have a phenomenon. Now you've got guys everywhere discussing the merits of moss as a groundcover.

You've got men (and women) traveling across the country to sit in a gazebo, have a beer, and watch the trains run through the landscape.

Railroad gardening may be the perfect way for men to take back the garden: just hitch it to a locomotive. The plants have a new purpose; they become scenery. And the gardener has a new quest: finding the perfect plants for tiny scenes, for they have to be the right size and scale to fit in.

The train layout provides a guy with a way to bring order and a certain logic to his garden. He's totally in control of his little world. And he gets to play with trains and little buildings. Finally he can satisfy his childhood dollhouse envy. In the railroad garden the world is simple and manageable. It's populated by small-town storekeepers, tiny schoolhouses, village greens, and shops. You never see a skyscraper or a Walmart or a Starbucks in a railway village. Instead, there's a general store and an ice cream parlor. And if you spend enough time and energy working on your railroad, you can almost shrink down and enter that simpler world.

Usually these guys enter this world via the train, not through the garden. Take Roger Clarkson, for example. He owns a model shop, and he has constructed a huge, elaborate, incredibly detailed HO-gauge train setup in the basement of his house in Riverside. And the train layout in his yard is even more impressive. In fact, this outdoor railroad has put Roger's house on the map. He hosts half a dozen tours of his garden every year, welcoming as many as three hundred people at a time. People call and ask for his open-house schedule months in advance so that they can plan their vacations around it.

Covering thousands of square feet, this railroad garden has ponds, streams, bridges, trestles, even a three-foot-tall hydroelectric dam. The streetlights are electric. There are telegraph poles, stores, shops, churches, miniature peo-

Ice plant makes a perfect ground cover for a miniature California railroad.

109

ple. A half-dozen trains snake through a perfectly trimmed landscape of dwarf conifers, arborvitae, and annual flowers. The locomotives are equipped with realistic digital sound.

"If we crank the sound up all the way, the neighbors think there's a real train coming through," Roger says. He and his wife, Faith, work together to keep the place landscaped.

"Our knowledge of gardening is not great," he admits. "We put in things that are pretty. We put in things that we know are going to last. If they die, we replace them." The landscaping definitely takes a back seat to the structures. "You can't have flowers everywhere because that wouldn't be realistic," he says. "In a real railroad there aren't flowers everywhere."

But they enjoy the gardening. "It's good therapy. You get to working in the garden and you just forget about everything else."

Roger and Faith work hard to make their back-yard world a whimsical, happy place. "We have a lot of comical signs and things," Roger says. "We do it to make people laugh. We have a Disney World setup over there with the castle. We have an old woman in a shoe."

Underneath, though, it's all business. This place is built to last, with hundreds of yards of trucked-in soil and fill, and the tracks constructed on a steel and concrete foundation. All told, Roger has spent about $100,000 creating this world. This is one serious garden railway.

Then there's Doug Johnson, who was just looking for something to do in his retirement. He and his wife, Joanne, had begun landscaping their hillside property in East Montpelier when he came across an article about garden railroads in a magazine. He showed it to Joanne, and they decided to give it a try.

Model trains had always been special to them. For Doug, it started when he was a kid, when his parents got him a train set for Christmas. Years later he and Joanne continued the tradition with their three children, setting up a huge train set for the holidays every year. For the Johnson family, as for many people, trains symbolized celebration, holiday, and, especially, family.

So in 1992 Doug and Joanne bought a G-scale train engine, a few cars and some track and started setting up a small loop. "We laid the track right on the lawn," Doug explains, "and then we would fight about where we wanted it. So we would change it three or four times before we agreed."

Garden railroading is often a couples' activity, as it was for the Johnsons until Joanne died. "I took care of the construction and the digging," Doug says. "She concerned herself with the flowers. I took charge of the shrubs." She taught him about using smaller plants. "I learned from my wife to be concerned with the color and shape of the foliage. Sometimes we didn't give a damn about the flowers. The flowers don't last for long anyway."

They continued to bicker about what should go where. "My wife eventually admitted that wherever there was an open space, she would put a flower in," Doug says. "So in our first section you couldn't even walk around without trampling on plants."

Trains and gardens don't always fit together seamlessly. There's a constant tension between growing plants and moving trains. "The main thing you have to learn is to allow enough space," Doug says. "You have to leave room around the track to keep the track clean and to let you to get in there to take care of the flowers."

And you have to be ruthless in curtailing wayward plants. "The first year we put the track down, I wouldn't pull anything out," Doug says. "If something was growing across the tracks, I wouldn't even pull it up." But he has changed. "Now I reach for the Roundup," he chuckles. That herbicide is a regular accompaniment to many train

After retiring from the insurance business in 1992, Doug Johnson combined his two loves: gardening and model trains. He has constructed an elaborate outdoor train setup in his yard in central Vermont.

A single train engine may cost thousands of dollars — as much as a landscape full of plants — but the equipment is virtually indestructible. The tracks can remain in place year-round.

gardens. "In fact, there's a fellow designing himself a tank car to put Roundup in to drip alongside the track!"

There's also the problem of plants growing out of scale. "I had two dwarf Alberta spruce that I put in at the start," Doug says. "But they got to be almost six feet tall, so I had to dig them up and move them. Now they're near the Alpine village." He's looking for miniature spruce to take their place.

Once the tracks have been laid, most of the railroader's energy is spent looking for just the right plants. In that way a guy is united with every other train gardener out there. The quest for the perfect miniature plant — one that is approximately the same scale as the trains and villages and buildings — is not easy.

"In my regular gardens now, I just want stuff to grow," Doug says. "As long as it grows and fills up space, okay. But in the train garden, I've got to be specific as to what I'm growing. I need the smaller stuff. Dwarf conifers, such as spruce and cedars, are good. Creeping ground covers like thyme, heathers, moss, and sedum all work."

If you're not too critical, if you squint from a distance, the scale of the plants seems almost right. But most of these gardeners can't resist the color offered by petunias, marigolds, pansies, violas, or columbines, which often look like giant mutant plants, maybe the result of a nuclear power–plant meltdown, beside the trains and villages.

"This kind of gardening absolutely focuses you on the plant selection," Doug says. "You look for smaller stuff, but if some gets large, well, there's a lot of astilbe out there in my garden, the purple astilbe, and the pink, and the red. God, they're gorgeous. Now they're this high, but gee, y'know? And the columbine in front is probably a little large, but it's colorful. And the ajuga just runs rampant, it takes over. So I built a stone wall and contained it in there."

After a trip to the LGB model factory in Germany, Doug was inspired to build a new spur to an Alpine village at the top of a hill on his property.

You have to keep pruning and training to keep the plantings in bounds. "At the flower show one year, there was a guy who had heather growing all over," Doug says. "It was beautiful. And I said, 'I've got heather out there, but it's growing too high.' 'Yeah,' he says, 'but you can cut it back.' Rosemary makes good trees, and you can buy it at any nursery. Parsley, too."

Garden railroads have their own set of challenges, similar to but a bit different from those of conventional gardening. There's the mulch/ground cover issue, always a hot topic when garden railroaders—or is it railroad gardeners?—get together.

"One of the big problems is..." Doug begins, then catches himself. "Well, let's face it, there aren't really any *big* problems. But one is figuring out how to keep the dirt from splashing up on the buildings. It's important to keep the buildings clean."

That leads to the first part of Doug's two-part formula

A MAN'S GARDEN

(*Opposite*) Garden railroaders soon learn that "miniature" is a relative term. In Johnson's garden, miniature sunflowers tower over the trains.

(*Above*) Rosemary and curly parsley are just about the right scale for make-believe trees. Miniature violas are a bit large, but no one in the garden railroad world seems to mind very much.

for railway success. It's easy, he says. It just requires two things: "Mulch and money." "We use a lot of cocoa-bark mulch," he says. And it works fine. "One year I had my town square just sitting on grass. Well, that works. But then I've got to cut the grass. We're talking maintenance here." He figures it's enough to have to mow the rest of the yard around the railroad without having to pull out a miniature lawnmower to mow inside the village.

Doug seems to belong to the more relaxed school of railroad gardening. He's not after pure authenticity. His buildings and bridges mix different time periods. Other people's setups are a bit more, well, compulsive. "You've got a lot of different people from a lot of different disciplines who get into garden railroading," he says. "Lots of them come from HO gauge, where they're very fussy. You've got a lot of craftsmen and rivet counters. Those are the one who say, 'That model of that train isn't right; there are thirteen rivets on the engine where there are only sup-

(Above) Electric power to run the trains is supplied through the track, which is completely waterproof and "hardy" enough to be left outdoors all year, even in Vermont.

(Opposite) Garden railroaders are constantly on the lookout for the perfect ground cover. Stone and moss cover the tiny town square in Doug's setup.

posed to be six, and the wheel is an eighth of an inch too big.'"

Besides mulch and money and miniature plants, one other element is vital to model railroading: rock. "We all use a lot of rocks," Doug says. "The track wants to be as flat as it can be, so you have to do something else to create the impression of height and depth in the landscape." He has used the natural slope of his property to create a railroad spur to the Alpine village up the hill from the main "town." The village is planted with a few conifers but little else.

"My wife said, 'You're not gonna put a lot of stuff in that village. It's gonna be plain.' I have to admit my wife was right that one time," he says with a smile.

Though his railroad looks complete, as the track circles the gazebo, runs over a trestle, through a lumber yard and sawmill, over a covered bridge modeled after the bridge in nearby Wolcott, around the town square, and up to the Alpine village, Doug still has big plans. He abandoned the idea of creating a Wild West town up on the hill, but now he has bigger fish to fry.

He's talking about damming up a stream to make a pond big enough to hold a ferryboat that will carry engines across to a miniature lime kiln on the other side. That should really impress the other railway guys.

Bragging rights are a big part of the attraction of the garden railroad. The hobby gives these guys a chance to get together and compare notes. One common element in all the garden railroads is a platform, deck, or, preferably, a gazebo where the guys can sit and chew the fat while they run the trains.

In the end, garden railroads are all about men getting together for a common purpose, even if that purpose is to run a toy train through a field of oversized pansies. As Doug Johnson says. "We get so involved, we sometimes forget that we are playing with toy trains. Building your own town from scratch makes you feel like you are lord of your universe."

A MAN'S GARDEN

THE CARETAKER

DAVID ALFORD

DURANGO, COLORADO

THE COTTAGE GARDEN STANDS OUT like a neon sign in front of the Blue Lake Ranch. It's beautiful, for sure, but it seems out of place in the high desert of Durango. At 7,400 feet, the native vegetation is monochromatic sagebrush and cactus. But this garden looks as if someone has thrown as many colors as possible on a canvas.

Come by any time between the end of June, when the snow has finally melted, and October, when it blankets the earth again, and you'll see the field in front of the main guest house ablaze with blooms. There are larkspur, sweet peas, poppies, and old-fashioned petunias.

How did all of these eastern temperate plants take root in the wild west? David Alford will tell you. He could blame it on his idyllic childhood. He was one of those kids who was always willing to take an injured animal home with him, the one who collected stuff nobody else wanted and made something with it. He was the kind of kid who

(Opposite) David Alford has an iris problem: he loves them too much. He couldn't resist planting hundreds and hundreds of nursery castaways — so many that he decided to start a dig-your-own-iris business.

(Above) A home-grown prairie surrounds Blue Lake Ranch. It's bursting with the colors of such plants as monarda, echinacea, and rudbeckia.

119

David remembers his grandmother harvesting armloads of peonies from her garden in upstate New York. He's recreated that memory in the high desert of Colorado.

grows up to be a social worker or an innkeeper or a gardener. As it happens, David is all three.

Now, just barely on the far side of fifty, David doesn't look (or act) his age. He's still tall and thin. His curly hair is still a bit long; his sandy mustache looks as if it's been in place since the sixties.

David speaks fondly of his childhood back in western New York State. It's not easy to find someone who speaks fondly of living in Buffalo, as he does. Then again, he's not living there anymore. Still, when he thinks of his childhood, he thinks of his grandmother's garden. And there's no question that he has tried to re-create that garden, especially the feeling of being in it, here, two thousand miles away.

"I grew up in a family that always had inspiring gardens," he says. "I have wonderful memories of my grandparents' acres and acres of old-fashioned gardens along the shore of Lake Erie, where they grew digitalis and dogwood and peonies by the armload. Having a garden now connects me with some memories from my golden childhood growing up with cousins on a family farm and living grandparents and a lake to swim in all day long."

Like many men, David had a hunger to recapture those carefree times. And, like many men, he had to suffer through garden withdrawal for quite some time as he worked at his career and the rest of his life.

"I went to Smith College in Massachusetts," he says, "and after I earned my master's degree I took a field placement as a social worker in Denver."

Even though Colorado was a long way from where he grew up, David felt at home right away. "I felt like I had died and gone to heaven when I arrived, what with the mountains and blue sky and fresh air." The only thing missing was a garden.

He lived in Denver through the early seventies. Then one day his roommate returned from a trip and said, "Let's move to Durango."

Alford's not afraid to use old-fashioned and perhaps over-looked flowers, such as petunias. Here they create a wave of color running through double rows of calendula.

And they did. Just like that. They packed up and found a house to buy for $20,000. Immediately David started attacking the hard caliche clay soil.

"I got behind a rototiller and just went," he explains. "I just love soil preparation. That's one of my favorite parts of gardening."

So he would dig a little, plant a little, and after a number of years passed, he opened a country inn. He put hollyhocks around the entrance to the main lodge, poppies near the fence, and huge drifts of echinacea in a rear garden. Now there are calendula and liatris, and clematis climbing the fence.

He admits that at first his garden style was a bit restrictive. "I had planted everything in straight rows, and a friend came over and took a look at the compulsively neat gardens and said, 'Dave, I had no idea you had such problems with your toilet training in your youth.' After that, I decided no more straight rows."

And he's stuck with his pledge. Today it would be hard to find a single straight row on the entire twenty acres. What's important to him is color, great masses of it. Beyond the highly visible cottage gardens there are several other large-scale plantings, from meadows painted rusty orange with gaillardia to bulb gardens. "I love mass plantings," he says. "Gardening is just a total visual experience for me." And when he plants bulbs, he plants a *lot*.

"I'm like a squirrel in the fall, digging holes all over," he says. "Y'know, I had a friend who was a triathlete, and he had a heart attack during one of his events, and it made

(Opposite) Alford wants the guests who stay at Blue Lake Ranch to feel integrated into the gardens. Have a seat here and you'll find yourself swallowed up by the prairie.

(Above) Never mind that the climate at 7,000 feet in the Rockies is the opposite of that on the shores of Lake Erie in New York, where David grew up; by force of will he has coerced familiar eastern flowers, such as sweet peas, to bloom here.

me realize that life is so short. Now, where I used to plant one daffodil, I plant ten."

Even as an adult, he's still adopting strays. But now those orphans are plants that need a home. And David will never turn one away. "I have a friend who was in the cut-flower peony business," he says. "He had to give it up because of a divorce. And he didn't know what to do with the plants. So I said I would take them." That was easier said than done. "I dug up 500 peonies. Brought them all home

and broke the wheel off my truck on the way. Then I divided them and wound up planting 2,500 peonies."

What is he going to do with them? They could eventually become a business. But for now "I just want to see them bloom," he says. "That would be enough for me."

That field of peonies pales beside his iris. "I have an iris problem," he admits. And what is it? "Instead of planting fifty, I planted twenty thousand."

That iris overload started a few years ago when he vis-

(Above). It's hard to imagine a nursery that is more attractive than Alford's iris patch. He allows customers to dig them while the plants are in full bloom.

(Opposite) David favors old-fashioned flowers — single hollyhocks and this strain of extremely fragrant, nonhybrid petunias.

ited a small nursery that sold dig-your-own iris for four bucks a pop. "I asked the owner how many they sold every year, and when she said fifteen thousand, I did a little quick math and I said, Wow, I can do that.

"At about the same time, I was talking to Jack Durance, a local iris hybridizer who told me that he threw out a lot of unnamed tubers. And I said, 'Don't throw them out. I'll plant them.' So we kept planting the throwaways in a field out back for a couple of years. Eventually Jack retired and

gave us his entire collection. So we planted them all, and now we have our own dig-your-own-iris business. We open to the public in the second or third week of June, and people come in and dig the irises in full bloom. The irises hardly even know they've been dug."

He is still planting new gardens around the property. "I just added a totally new garden at one of our new guest casitas," he says. "I put in a wonderful dwarf penstemon, some potentilla, and a gorgeous 'Black Night' spirea. Then

124

I planted plenty of culinary sage just for foliage. And I put in a Russian olive. The gray looks wonderful against the red adobe stucco."

As David walks the property with guests, he can't help but notice that it's a crazy quilt of colors and garden styles. But he doesn't apologize for that. "As I've gardened I've had periodic passions," he says. Sometimes they work out, and sometimes they don't. A case of the latter was snow in summer. "Do yourself a favor and don't plant that stuff,"

he says. "It's just too invasive." He's tilling up a huge patch of it and replacing it with, of all things, a lawn. David will never be accused of politically correct gardening.

David's latest garden passion is southwestern native plants, including yucca, cholla, prickly pear, and tiny pincushion cactus. How does he plant them in among the blooms of the cottage gardens?

"Very carefully, with heavy leather gloves," he says.

125

Button says that even though Vita Sackville-West disapproves of twin borders flanking a path, he doesn't care. He isn't interested in what others think of his garden as long as he's happy with it.

A MAN'S GARDEN

It's not hard to figure out why Olympic gold-medal figure skater Dick Button calls the upright blooms of this amaranth "response to the judges."

THE ENTERTAINER

DICK BUTTON

NORTH SALEM, NEW YORK

Dick Button is spinning like a top at the center of his fifty-acre property in New York's Hudson Valley. As he points out the features of the landscape, he can't resist skipping from one to another. His excitement is infectious.

Button, short and stocky, with a trim, dark beard, dressed in khaki shorts, polo shirt, and battered baseball cap, seems far younger than his seventy years.

If it's possible to use the word "scurry" to describe the movement of a compact, muscular, graceful man, that might be how to describe Dick Button leading a tour of his garden. He is in a hurry to show it all. There are the obvious and obligatory plantings: the twin perennial borders, the pool garden, the crab apple allee, the vegetable garden. But he's really interested in helping you discover the more subtle features, the ones that require a little work, a little luck, and the right timing to appreciate. Such as the way the light strikes a certain urn, or the shadow cast by a bench, or the shape of a single tree in a distant meadow.

Talk with Dick Button for a while, and he makes it clear that this place centers on the small pond in the valley that splits the property. You can't always see the pond, it's true, but you catch the glint of water out of the corner of your eye as you wander. The importance of the pond is totally appropriate for Button, arguably the most famous American figure skater of all time. Two-time Olympic gold-medal

Button's borders are designed to highlight bright colors, such as the oranges and yellows of heliopsis and helianthus, in the summer and soften to the blues and grays of asters in the fall.

There was no room for tennis courts on the ridge that runs through Button's property, so he installed a bocce court instead and flanked it with a crabapple allee.

winner, skating analyst par excellence, producer of professional skating events, Dick got his start some sixty years ago skating on a small pond in New Jersey. He's come almost full circle.

Today, most people know Button as a television commentator. If you've ever watched figure skating on TV, you've heard him deconstruct a skater's program with a well-chosen word. He's known for his insight and his restraint. He doesn't fill the airwaves with chatter. Instead, he sits back and lets the program unfold, commenting only when it's warranted. In a way, his broadcasts are like his gardens. He's always been able to find and appreciate the artistic merits of a performance, pointing out how it builds musically to a climax, or how it has the elements of drama: a beginning, middle, and end. One might say the same about his garden.

Chronologically, the borders were the beginning for Button, who came to gardening late in life. For the first few years he lived at his country house, he grew only a small vegetable garden. Then, about ten years ago, he put in the borders. He admits he has learned a lot since then.

"I suppose if I were doing it over, I wouldn't do these borders the same way," he says as he walks the path between them. In fact, he laughs about the mistakes he's made. "I was reading Jane Brown's book about Vita Sackville-West, and I had to put it down and stop reading at one point because she said, 'Vita would never have two perennial borders flanking a walk. Vita would never have an arbor, or a fountain.' Those are all things that I have. But I planned my border out long before I ever heard of Vita Sackville-West."

It might not have made a difference, either. Button is a

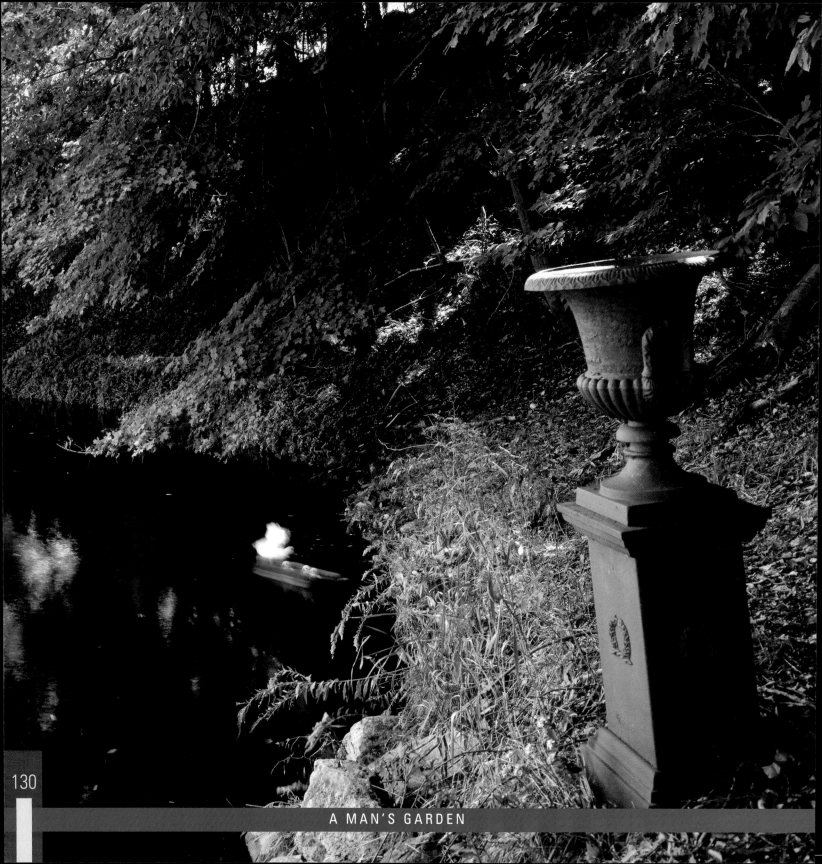

(Opposite) The pond in the valley is the focal point around which everything revolves. An urn is placed so that low sunlight illuminates it at the end of the day.

(Right) New England asters take over the borders in the fall. Button affectionately refers to the two planters filled with sedum as "Peggy Fleming with an afro."

stubborn guy. He likes to do things his own way. He did have some help, though, from landscape designer Page Dickey. "She lives around the corner," Dick says, "and she designed the original pool garden."

He listened to her advice and followed it. Well, some of it. "To her credit, when I would drop by and say, 'Page, I didn't do it this way, I did it that way,' she would just smile and laugh. What I did was not necessarily right, but that's not the point. I was having fun with it." And that is the point of the whole garden experience, says Button—fun.

Fun. Joy. Even glee. They are all evident here. Button has a mischievous twinkle in his eye as he leads a tour of the garden. Start at the beginning of the twin borders, which are guarded by twin planters in the shape of a woman's head. He insists they represent his broadcasting partner, gold-medal skater Peggy Fleming. The year they

were filled with succulents, he called them Peggy Fleming with an afro. The year before that they were planted with nasturtiums, and he called them Peggy Fleming on a bad-hair day.

Two elements that you see everywhere in his garden are skating references and humor. Walking by the border, he shows you what he calls an oxalis ball, an obvious pun on the name of the skater Oksana Baiul. Or he points to the huge red amaranth plume that looks like nothing so much as a hand with the middle finger raised. "And that," he says, "I call 'response to the judges'. Actually, the whole place is my 'F——— You' garden. If you don't like it, that's your problem."

That's an attitude you'll find only in a man's garden. But this is not just any man's garden. Button has had enough success to know that he doesn't have to impress anyone

(Left) An old barn, festooned with morning glories, remains from the property's farm days. Fling open the door, and you see a perfectly framed view of the valley beyond.

(Opposite) The pool garden was Button's first grown-up garden effort. He got plenty of advice but ignored most of it to plant what appealed to him.

with his peonies or roses. A plant out of place is not a catastrophe for a man who gardens only for his own pleasure.

Button appreciates that the garden grants him a refuge from the spotlight. "In skating, for me, everything is deadly serious. But gardening? That's just fun and games," he says. "It isn't my profession. And you know what? If I can't get to some garden chore, too bad. It's no big deal. But if I did that in my business world, if I didn't get my work done, I'd be a nervous wreck. I just really find gardening exceedingly satisfying. The frustrations are really exasperations, as opposed to business, where frustrations sound the death knell."

Even Sackville-West might approve of his borders now. It's hard not to like them. They're full, blowsy, cottage-gar-

deny, overflowing with flowers from spring until the fall frost. They're designed to evolve through the seasons.

"They start out with that pink plumy flower," Button says, then he apologizes for forgetting the botanical name. "I'm still thinking in terms of skaters' names and skating terminology," he explains.

"Then they progress through yellow and orange, the rudbeckia, heliopsis, and helianthus. "I can't really keep those last two straight," he admits, sotto voce. But he doesn't seem to care too much. When he's broadcasting a skating event, he would never trip over a tongue-twisting Russian name. That's the difference between his garden and his business.

"I'm beginning to add more salvia," he says. "I'm getting more color in here, so that it's a mass of yellow before it shifts to the blue of salvia, and the native asters that take

THE ENTERTAINER

Button has cut, pruned, mowed, and bush-hogged to find and reveal the best borrowed views from his property.

over in the fall. I really like those asters, because they're so carefree."

In fact, the entire border is built around his work schedule. "I'm so busy with skating in fall, I don't have time to plan out and think about planting spring bulbs. Spring is busy, too, so I don't get into the garden until late May and June. By then everybody else's garden is so glorious. It takes me all summer to catch up. In July I hear other gardeners saying they're so sick of their gardens, and I say,

'Goddamn it, it's only been two months, and you've had it?!'

Button is in it for the long term. He enjoys the slow, steady progression of the seasons. "To me gardening should be enjoyed like a long love-making process before that final chrysanthemum bursts," he says. "I hate it when the first frost comes and I lose the garden. That's the other reason I have so many asters, to extend the bloom as long as possible in the fall.

"There are still so many things I'd like to try. And they're usually the old-fashioned, time-honored things," he says as he tucks a wayward sunflower back into line. Again, he slips back into skating references. "A skater will go by and do a triple axel, and somebody will say, 'Wasn't that the most wonderful triple axel you ever saw?' and I go cross-eyed. I say, 'Oh, for Pete's sake, didn't you ever see David Jenkins in 1960?' Somebody will say, 'Wasn't that the most wonderful spin?' and I say, 'C'm'on, how about Ronnie Robertson in 1956, or what about that gal who wound up skating topless in Vegas? She has the best centering in the world.'"

With plants, he's not so jaded. He hasn't yet seen it all. That's one of the great things about gardening for him. "I'm still falling in love with plants that other people have discarded," Button says. "I don't want a coreopsis that's half as high as it should be. I don't want my hollyhocks to be three feet high with blossoms like powder puffs. I want the old-fashioned stuff, and I'm not even wild about those dark colors. They're interesting species that I want to see in somebody else's garden, not mine. And I have none of the snobbiness about using annuals."

To him, garden snobs are pretty much the same as skating snobs. There are certain types in every endeavor. There's the business guy and the financial guy, the perfectionist and the braggart.

"Somewhere out there, there's the Page Dickey or the

A rustic arbor hung with grapes frames a glimpse of the meadow beyond.

PHOTO
CREDITS

Courtesy of Howard Dill: 46, 47, 48, 50

Randall Friesen: iii top left, 2, 35, 36, 37, 38, 39, 42, 43, 44

Mick Hales: viii left, 1, 18, 19, 20 left, 20 right, 21, 22, 23, 24, 25, 126, 127, 128, 129, 130, 131, 132, 133, 134, 135, 136, 139

Alan Jakubeck: ii top right, 3, 88, 89, 90, 91, 92, 95

Doug Johnson: 112, 114, 115, 116, 117

Dency Kane, courtesy of *Country Gardens* magazine: iii bottom, 27, 28, 29, 31, 32 top, 32 bottom, 33

Robert Kourik: ii bottom right, 66, 67, 68, 69, 70, 71, 72, 74

Charles Mann: xii, 118, 119, 120, 121, 122, 123, 124, 125

Felder Rushing: ii left, 52, 53, 54, 55, 56, 57, 58, 59, 60, 61, 62, 65

Warren Schultz: ix right, 4, 7 left, 7 right, 8-9 middle, 9 right, 10, 86, 87, 106-107, 108, 109, 111, 113

Susan Seubert: iii top right, ix left, 76, 77, 78 top, 78 bottom, 79, 80, 82, 83, 84

Allison Mia Starcher: 6

Dominique Vorillon: 12 left, 12 right, 13, 14, 15, 16, 17

Virginia R. Weiler: iii right, 96, 97, 98, 99, 100, 101, 103, 104

photo by Emme Schultz

ABOUT THE AUTHOR

Warren Schultz is former editor-in-chief of *National Gardening Magazine* and features editor of *Garden Design*. He is the author of *A Man's Turf: The Perfect Lawn*. He lives and gardens in Essex Junction, Vermont, with his two daughters, Emme and Zea.